HISTORIC PHOTOS OF
ANN ARBOR

TEXT AND CAPTIONS BY
ALICE GOFF AND MEGAN COONEY

TURNER
PUBLISHING COMPANY

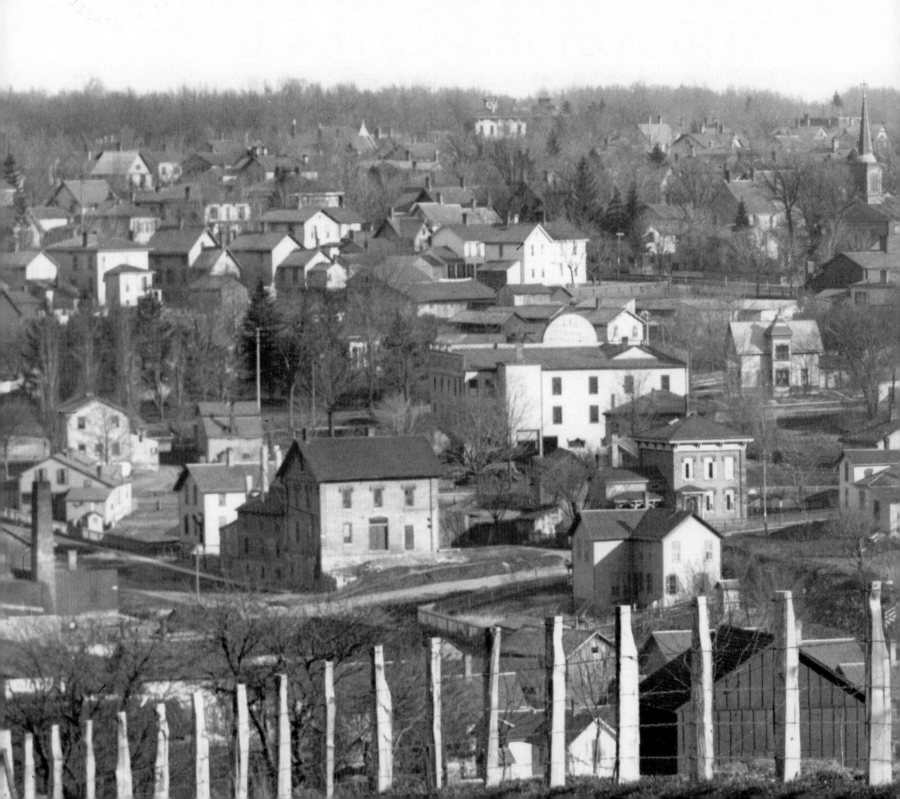

Panorama of Ann Arbor from Sunset Road (formerly Chubb Road) facing southeast, ca. 1890.

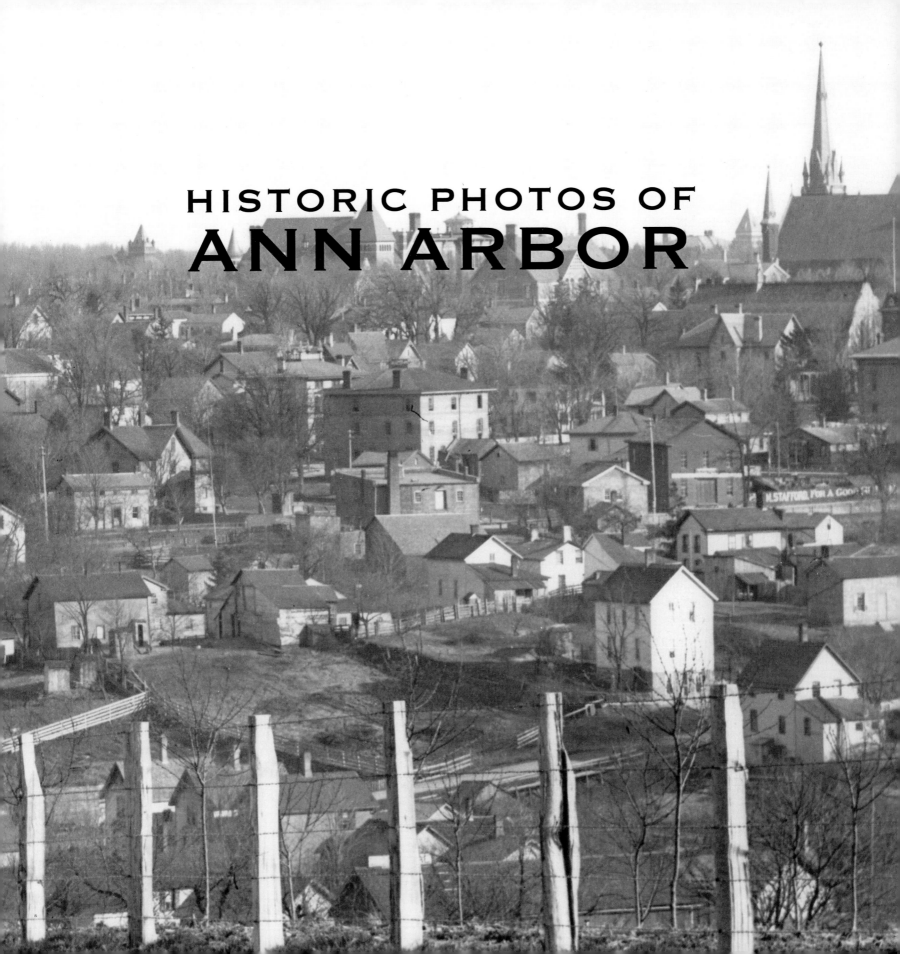

HISTORIC PHOTOS OF
ANN ARBOR

Turner Publishing Company
200 4th Avenue North • Suite 950   412 Broadway • P.O. Box 3101
Nashville, Tennessee 37219   Paducah, Kentucky 42002-3101
(615) 255-2665   (270) 443-0121

www.turnerpublishing.com

Historic Photos of Ann Arbor

Library of Congress Control Number: 2007929610

ISBN-13: 978-1-59652-389-0

Printed in the United States of America

07 08 09 10 11 12 13 14—0 9 8 7 6 5 4 3 2 1

Contents

A Navy recruiting officer and couple. Military recruiting was especially vigorous in Ann Arbor, with its high population of young people. In 1942, the University Regents established the Division for Emergency Training, aimed at students preparing for military service.

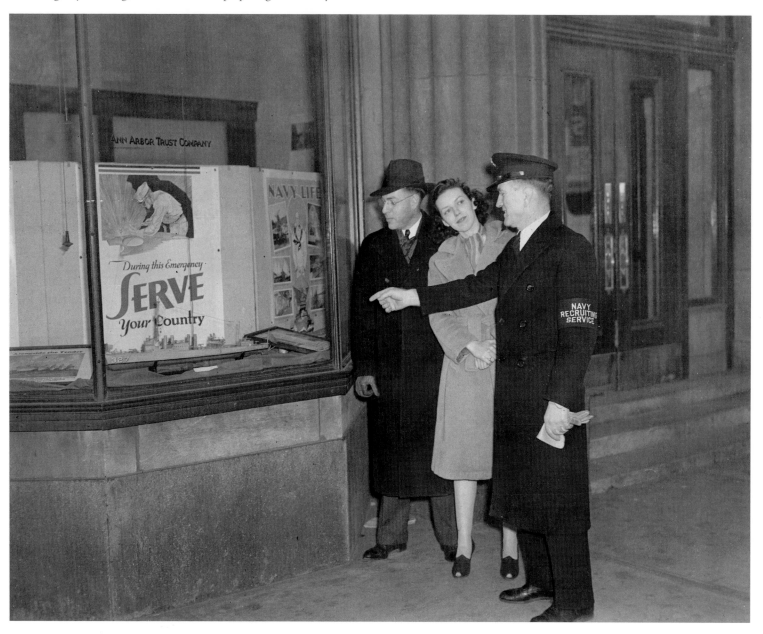

ACKNOWLEDGMENTS

This volume, *Historic Photos of Ann Arbor,* is the result of the cooperation and efforts of many individuals and organizations. It is with great thanks that we acknowledge in particular the Bentley Historical Library, University of Michigan, for their generous support.

The authors would also like to thank Karen Jania and the Bentley Historical Library Reference Staff for all of their help and support.

PREFACE

Ann Arbor has thousands of historic photographs that reside in archives, both locally and nationally. This book began with the observation that, while those photographs are of great interest to many, they are not easily accessible. During a time when Ann Arbor is looking ahead and evaluating its future course, many people are asking, How do we treat the past? These decisions affect every aspect of the city—architecture, public spaces, commerce, infrastructure—and these, in turn, affect the way that people live their lives. This book seeks to provide easy access to a valuable, objective look into the history of Ann Arbor.

The power of photographs is that they are less subjective than words in their treatment of history. Although the photographer can make decisions regarding subject matter and how to capture and present it, photographs do not provide the breadth of interpretation that text does. For this reason, they offer an original, untainted perspective that allows the viewer to interpret and observe.

This project represents countless hours of review and research. The researchers and writer have reviewed thousands of photographs in numerous archives. We greatly appreciate the generous assistance of the individuals and organizations listed in the acknowledgments of this work, without whom this project could not have been completed.

The goal in publishing this work is to provide broader access to this set of extraordinary photographs that seek to inspire, provide perspective, and evoke insight that might assist people who are responsible for determining Ann Arbor's future. In addition, the book seeks to preserve the past with adequate respect and reverence.

With the exception of touching up imperfections caused by the damage of time and cropping where necessary, no other changes have been made. The focus and clarity of many images is limited to the technology and the ability of the photographer at the time they were taken.

The work is divided into eras. Beginning with some of the earliest known photographs of Ann Arbor, the first section records photographs through the end of the nineteenth century. The second section spans the beginning of the twentieth century through World War I. Section Three looks at the years between the wars. The last section covers the World War II era to recent times.

In each of these sections we have made an effort to capture various aspects of life through our selection of photographs. People, commerce, transportation, infrastructure, religious institutions, and educational institutions have been included to provide a broad perspective.

We encourage readers to reflect as they go walking in Ann Arbor, strolling through the city, its parks, and its neighborhoods. It is the publisher's hope that in utilizing this work, longtime residents will learn something new and that new residents will gain a perspective on where Ann Arbor has been, so that each can contribute to its future.

—Todd Bottorff, Publisher

The west side of Main Street, between Huron and Washington streets, before 1862. The street's original plank sidewalk is visible, as well as hitching posts for horses and buggies. Pictured are Herman Schlotterbeck's confectionery and bakery, John W. Hunt's hardware store, C. H. Millen's dry goods store, and the printing office of the newspaper *Ann Arbor Argus*.

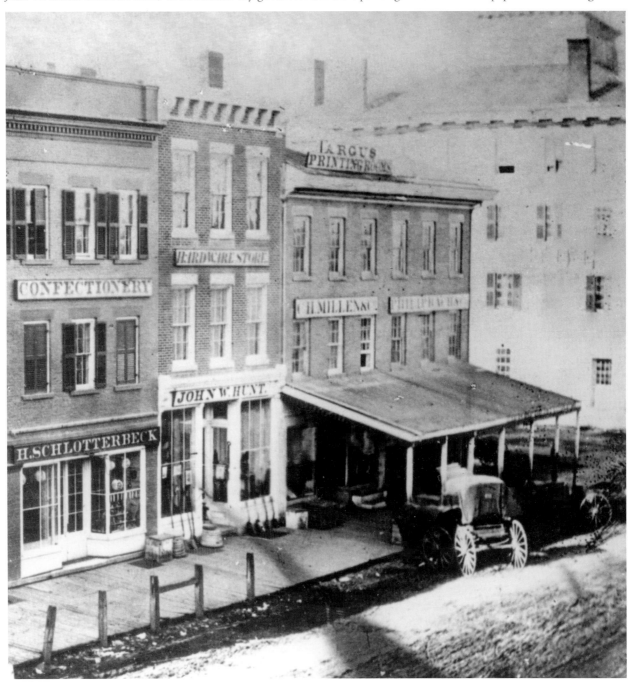

Growth of a University Town

(1860–1899)

The future looked very promising for the small frontier town of Ann Arbor in the first part of the nineteenth century. Founded in 1824 by Easterners John Allen and Elisha Rumsey (and as legend has it, named after their wives, both of whom were called Ann), Ann Arbor benefited from a number of lucky breaks. In 1827 it became the seat of Washtenaw County, receiving state funding and prestige as a result. In 1836, Ann Arbor lost the bid to become capital of the State of Michigan, but one year later won what may have turned out to be a larger prize. In 1837 the city became the new site for the University of Michigan, after it offered up forty acres for the campus, free of charge. In 1839, Ann Arbor also became a stop on the Michigan Central Railroad, making it a key transportation hub.

In the latter part of the century, Ann Arbor's population increased steadily, attracting not only settlers from the east, but also a large population of German immigrants. The townspeople established a local government, organized a volunteer fire department, and assembled a small police force. They built homes, churches, and schools, and operated flour mills, breweries, and tanneries. The first president of the University, Henry Philip Tappan, sought to create a university on the German model, and in his few years of tenure, he built many buildings on the 40-acre campus. Later presidents, most notably the third, James B. Angell (who was much beloved in Ann Arbor and held the post for thirty-eight years), dramatically expanded the curriculum and physical size of the university. By 1866 the student body had grown to 1,205, with many of the students veterans of the Civil War.

Both the university and the town of Ann Arbor experienced a construction and population boom after the Civil War. A number of impressive buildings were erected during this time, including the beautiful Second Courthouse, built in 1872, and the Italian villa–style fire station, built in 1882. The city also experienced an increase in the number of saloons, hotels, and commercial businesses lining its main streets. City services expanded—the first telephone exchange was installed in 1881, and in 1884 the first electric lights in town were switched on. A water and sewer system followed in 1885 and 1894, respectively. In 1890 an electric railway was introduced, connecting the university area at State Street with both downtown and the train depot. These new connections, combined with local mail delivery, changed the university area into another commercial center. By the end of the nineteenth century, Ann Arbor had grown from a small frontier village to a bustling university town, one perfectly described by the 1913 Civic Association motto "City of Knowledge and Homes."

On April 15, 1861, a crowd assembled at the old Courthouse to hear the university president, Henry Tappan, announce the firing on Fort Sumter and the beginning of the Civil War. Tappan urged the assembled townspeople to support President Lincoln and to form military companies, in preparation for the war. Huron Street is visible in the background.

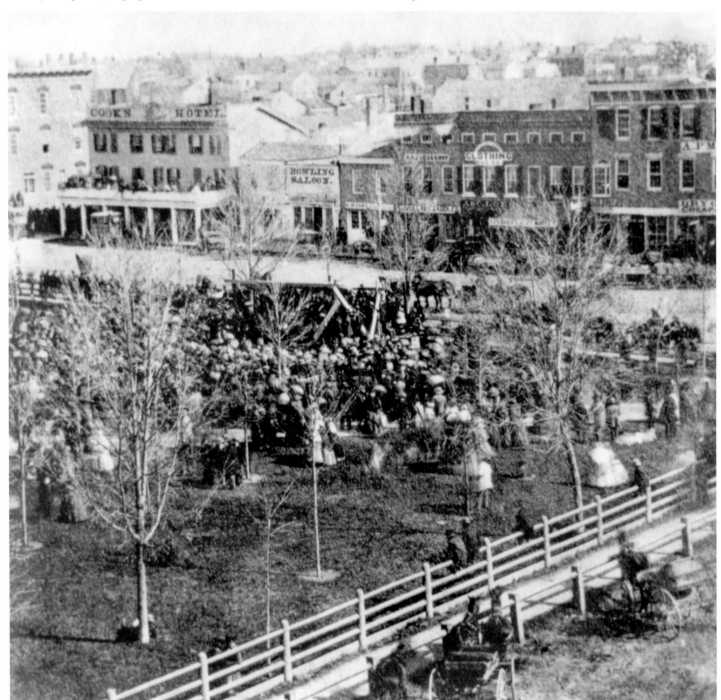

Soon after Tappan's April 15 announcement, three companies of student soldiers were formed. Pictured here are the captains of these companies in 1861: Charles K. Adams, Captain of the University Guards; Isaac H. Elliott, Captain of the Chancellor Greys; and Albert Nye, Captain of the Ellsworth Zouaves. Nearly half (78 out of 165) of the students who were matriculated between 1859 and 1862 went on to fight in the Civil War.

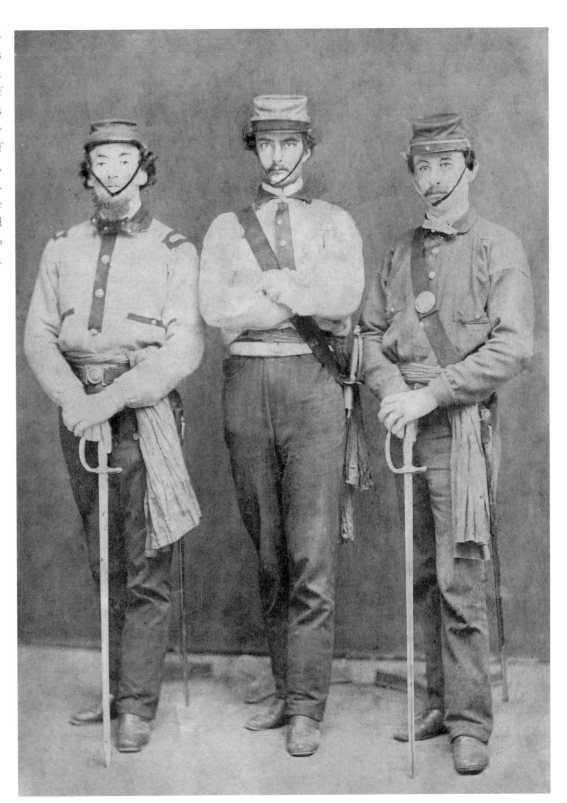

Located on the southwest corner of Main and Washington streets, the Hangsterfer Block (building) was erected in 1860 by German immigrant Jacob Hangsterfer. The First National Bank opened on the ground floor in 1863, joining Hangsterfer's confectionery. The third floor was a large ballroom (known as Hangsterfer Hall) that served as an important cultural center for many years, hosting popular dances, plays, and social gatherings.

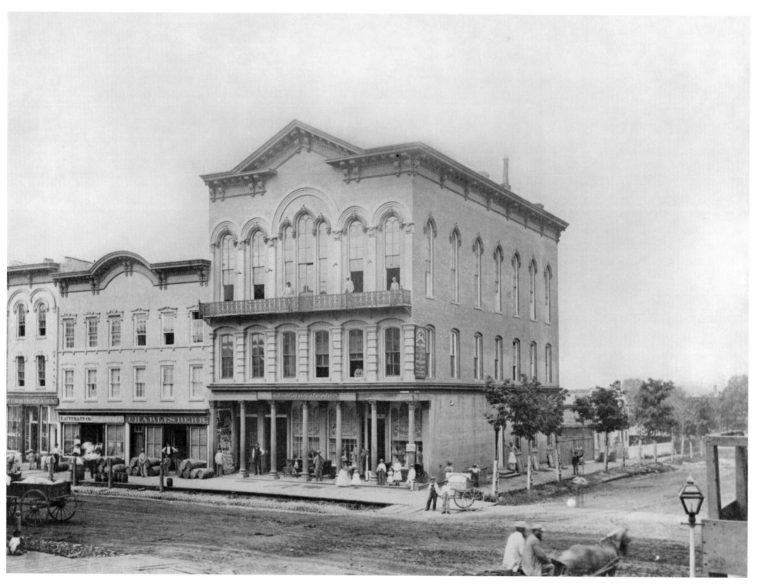

The Gregory House, ca. 1868. Located on the northwest corner of Huron and Main streets, the Gregory replaced the American Hotel in 1862. By 1872, Ann Arbor had eight hotels.

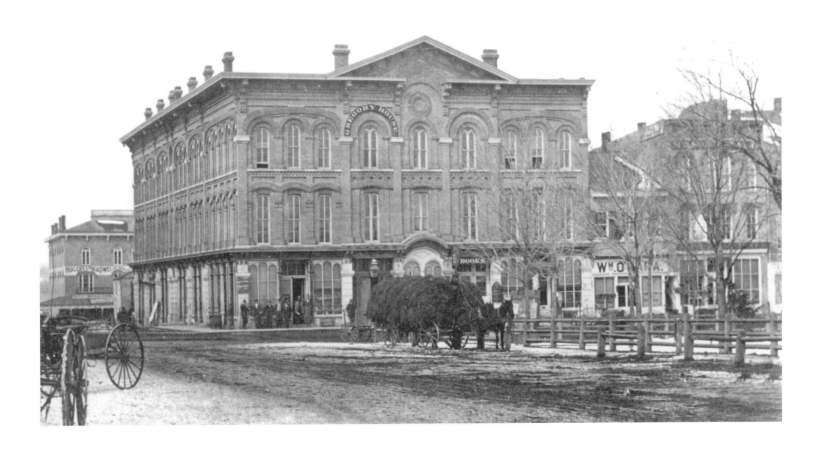

This 1865 photograph commemorates a game played between the Ann Arbor Baseball Club and their rivals, the Wahoo Baseball Club of Dexter, Michigan. Baseball became popular in Ann Arbor in the early 1860s, and in 1864 the university formed its first team.

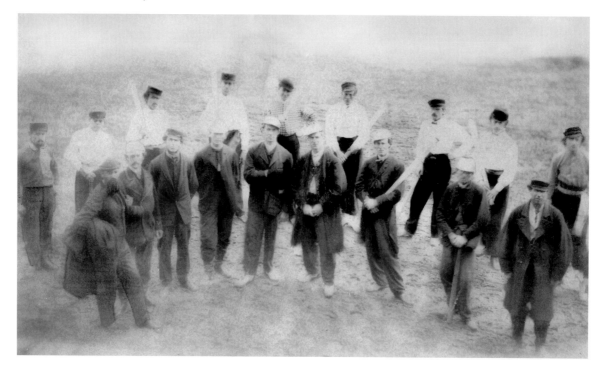

A view of Main Street northwest from Washington Street, ca. 1871-74. The Gregory House is visible at the corner of Huron and Main, and toward the foreground, Hutzel & Co.'s storefront advertises paints and oils.

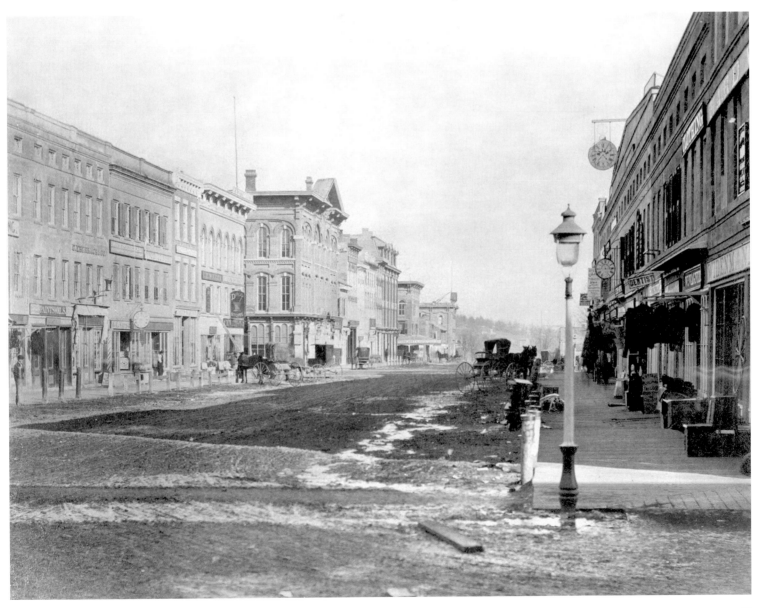

State Street facing south from Huron, including a view of the Methodist Episcopal Church, ca. 1870s. The Methodist Episcopal Church was built in 1866, and its distinctive steeple can be seen in many photographs from the era. With neither mail delivery nor trolley service, the State Street area was still somewhat residential during this time. In the foreground is the house of Ezra Seaman (editor of the *Ann Arbor Journal*) that then faced Huron.

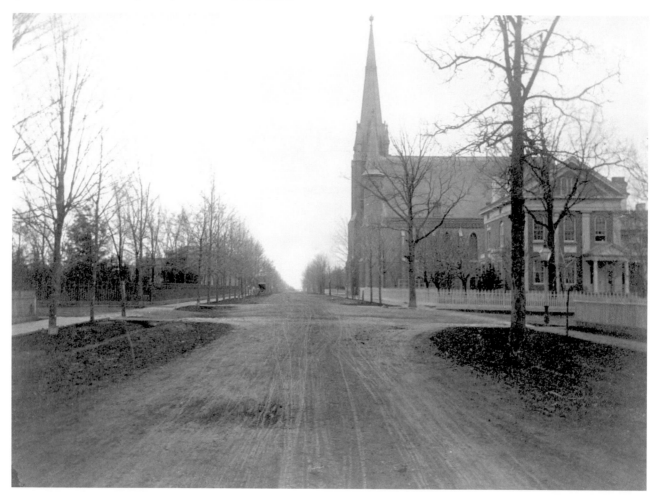

First Presbyterian Church, at Huron and Division streets, ca. 1865. Built in 1860, this structure housed the church until the congregation moved to their current location, on the eastern side of town on Washtenaw Avenue. In 1935 the building was demolished. The *Ann Arbor News* building is now located on the site.

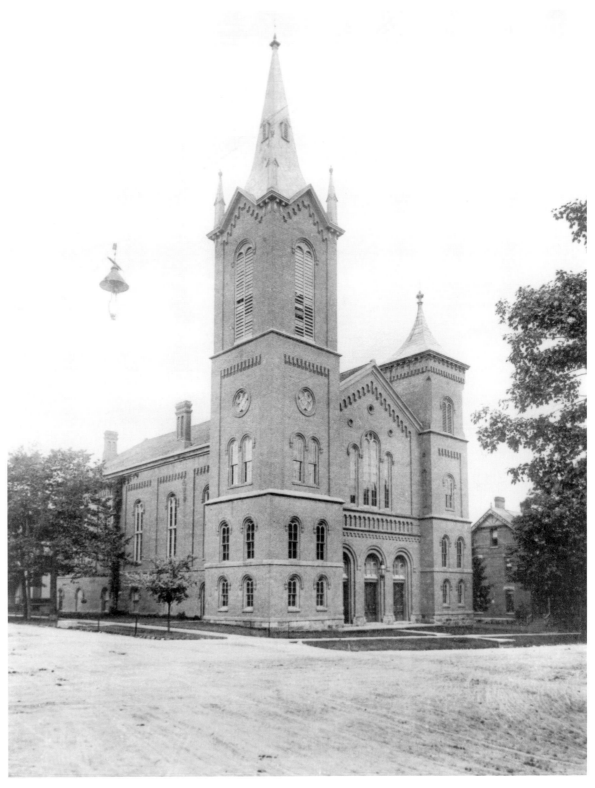

The Danforth and Royce houses at the corner of Ann Street and Fifth Avenue, ca. 1875. Attorney George Danforth built his Greek Revival home on this corner in 1845. The cabinetmaker James F. Royce then built his Italianate house next door in 1866, after coming to Ann Arbor in 1830 and operating a chair-making business for several decades. Royce's house still stands, though it is currently rented as apartments.

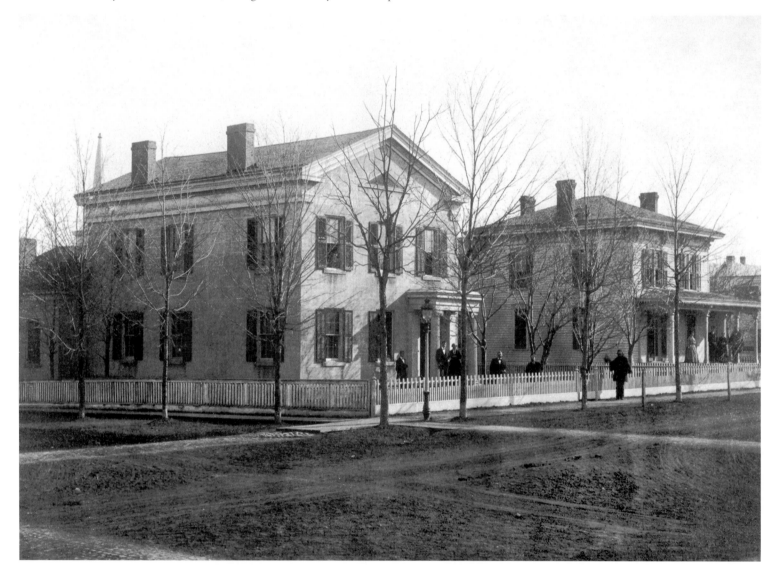

Ann Arbor's volunteer fire department, shown here in 1877, was organized in 1838 and replaced by a paid crew in 1888.

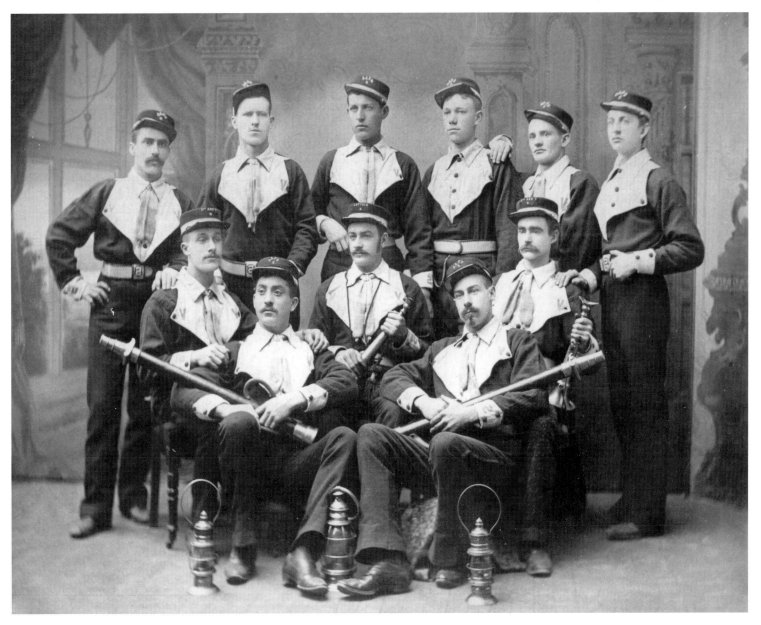

Drake's saloon and Jacob Haller's Jewelry on East Huron Street, ca. 1875. These shops were located in the thriving commercial district across the street from Ann Arbor's courthouse. Haller's Jewelry was established in 1858 and operated continuously for more than one hundred years.

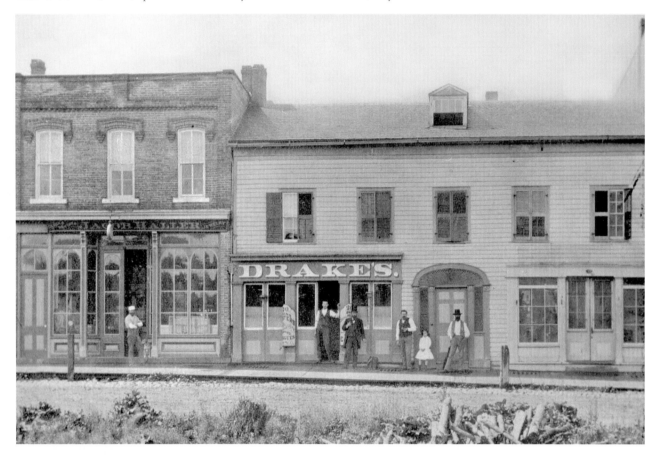

State Street facing north, from North University, ca. 1877. Visible here is the spire of the Methodist Church, at State and Washington, and the front of Sheehan's bookstore, which was the first of many bookstores in this area. University scholars (note their mortarboards) linger on the street.

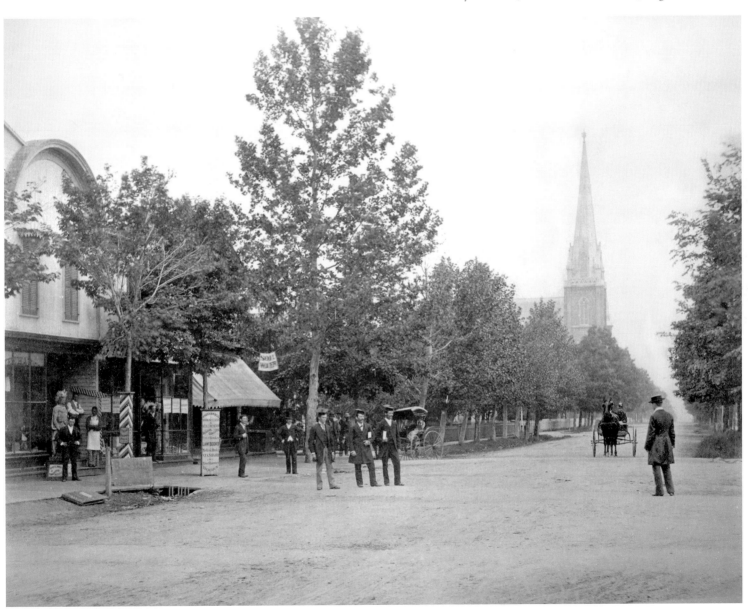

A view of the Huron River, facing east, ca. 1870. The area north of the river was still very rural at this time. The old Wall Street Bridge is visible in the distance.

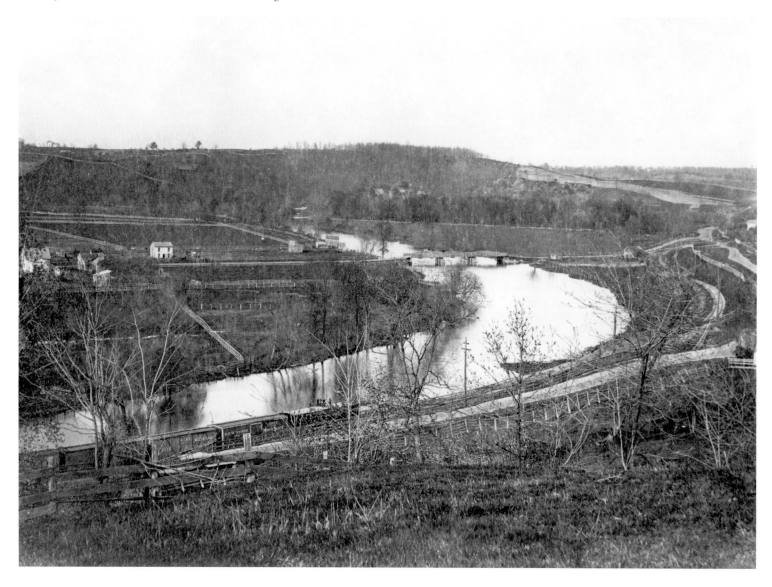

A beer delivery wagon in front of Binder's Saloon in 1872. Binder's saloon was located at 112 West Liberty, an area home to a number of German businesses. By 1872, there were forty-nine saloons in Ann Arbor, up from ten in 1860.

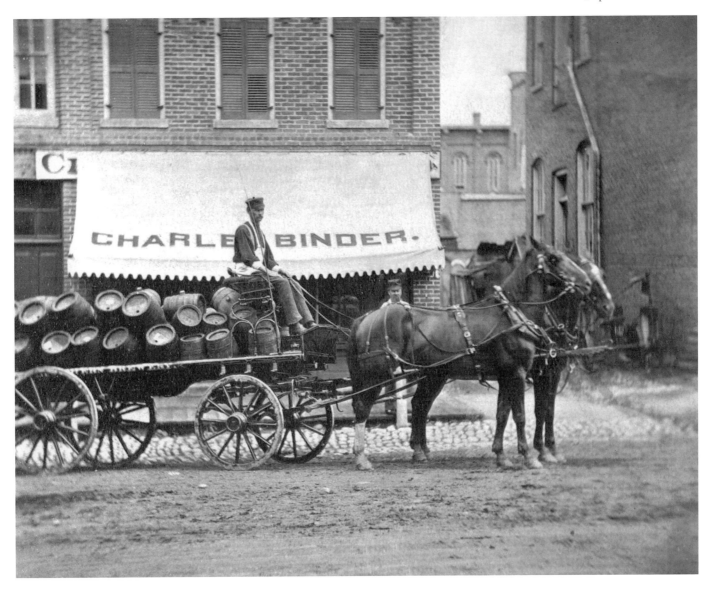

The John Nickels Meat Market, on State Street at North University, ca. 1870s. John Nickels operated this market from his home—he and his family lived in the back of the building. In 1915, the Nickels family built the Nickels Arcade on the same spot. The building at right housed a dining hall for students.

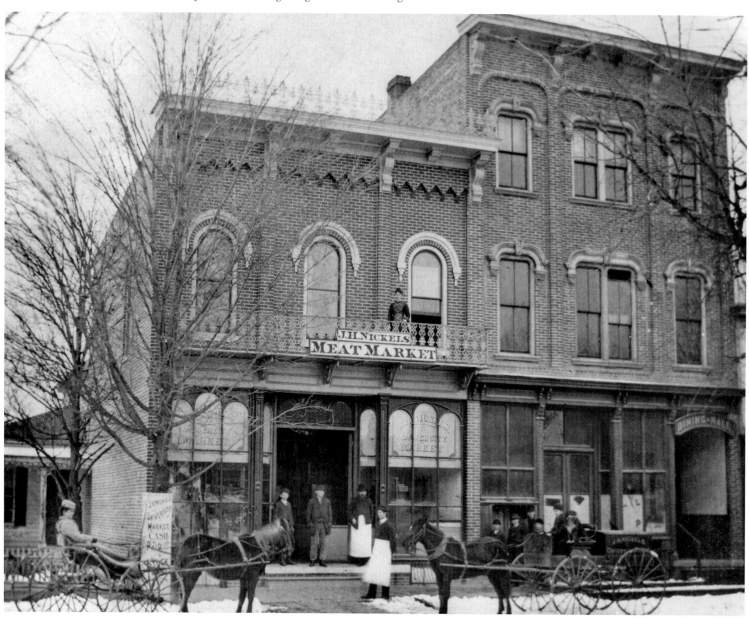

First German Church in Michigan, in 1881. In 1833, Pastor Friedrich Schmid founded this church for Ann Arbor's German immigrant population, who wanted to hear sermons in their native language. The church was located on the western side of town on Jackson Road, where Bethlehem Cemetery is today.

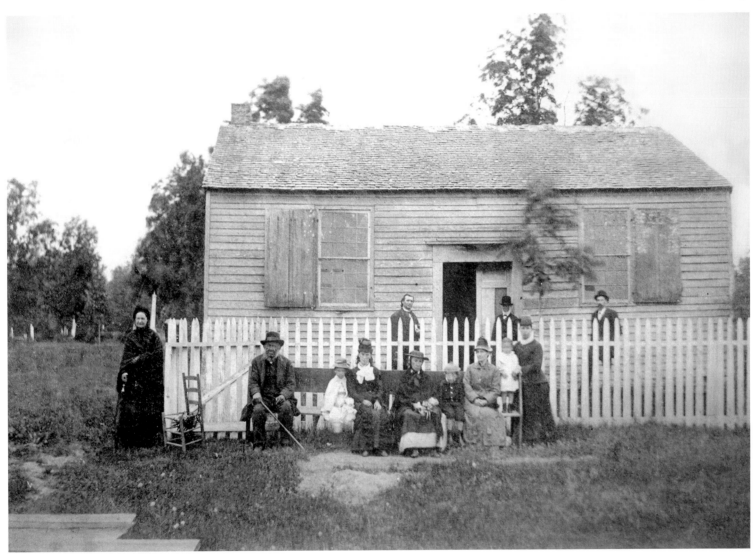

Ann Arbor from the northwest, in 1876. The 1866 Methodist Church can be seen to the left of the dome of University Hall, both visible on the skyline.

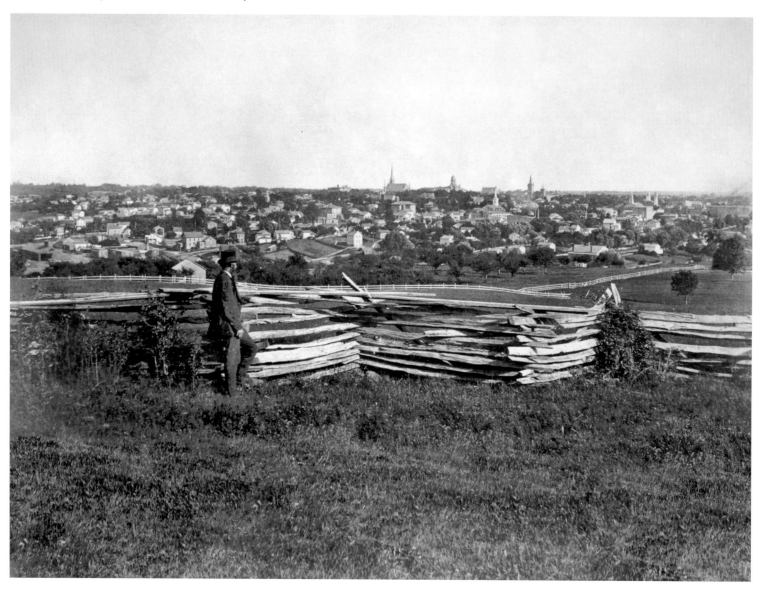

The Ann Arbor Organ Works, at the northwest corner of First and Washington streets, ca. 1872. The company was founded in 1872 by David F. Allmendinger, and originally located in these buildings, where he lived with his family. Eventually, the buildings in this complex were demolished to make way for large, brick factory buildings, where Allmendinger built not only organs, but also pianos. The brick buildings still stand today, taking up the entire block on First Street between Huron and Washington.

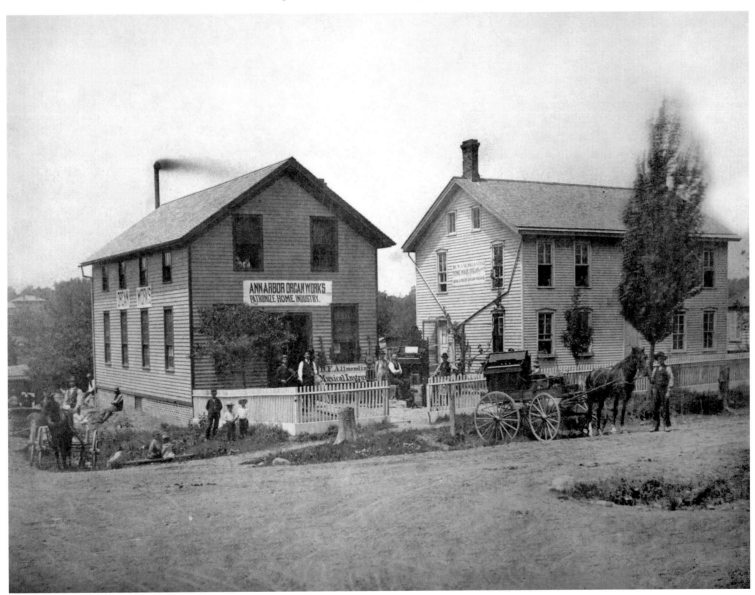

Shown here around 1885, this wooden railroad trestle was replaced with a
steel one in 1891, which subsequently collapsed in 1904.

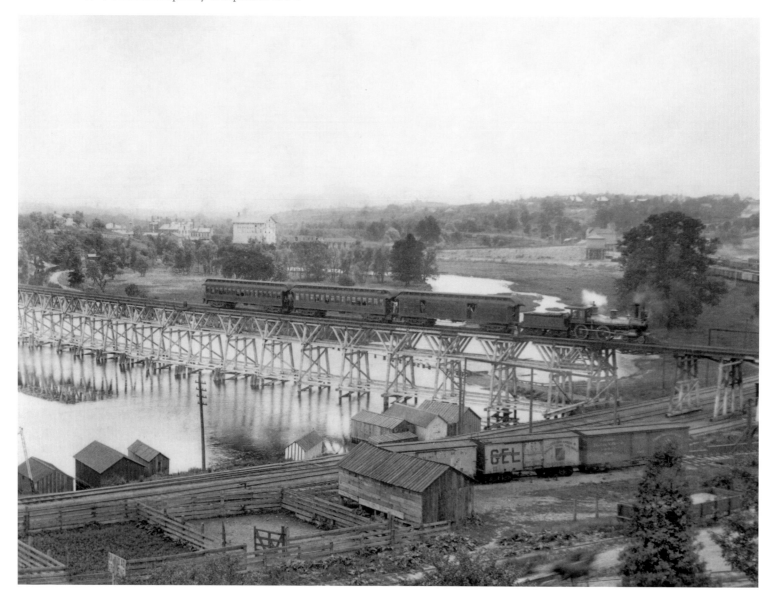

The Second
Courthouse was built
in 1878 and occupied
the entire block
bounded by Huron,
Main, Ann, and Fourth
streets. It was set in the
center of the block and
surrounded by grass
and shade trees. This
building replaced the
first courthouse, built
in 1834 on the same
block, facing south
from Ann Street, with
a large public square at
its front.

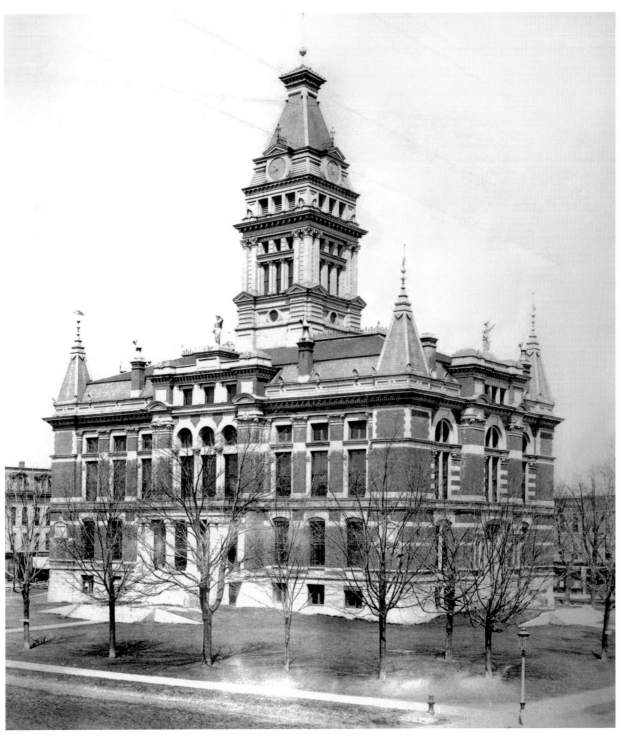

A seventh-grade class picture, June 14, 1884. In 1884 there were five public ward schools for the younger children of Ann Arbor.

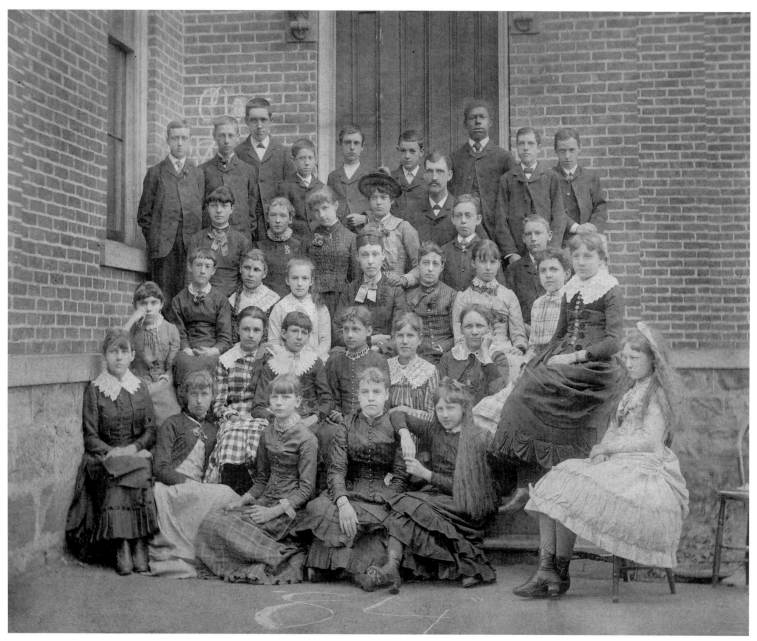

This icehouse was located on the Huron River, near Argo Pond. Harvested ice was stored near the river in icehouses like this one, and delivered during the warm weather months to businesses and private homes for use in iceboxes.

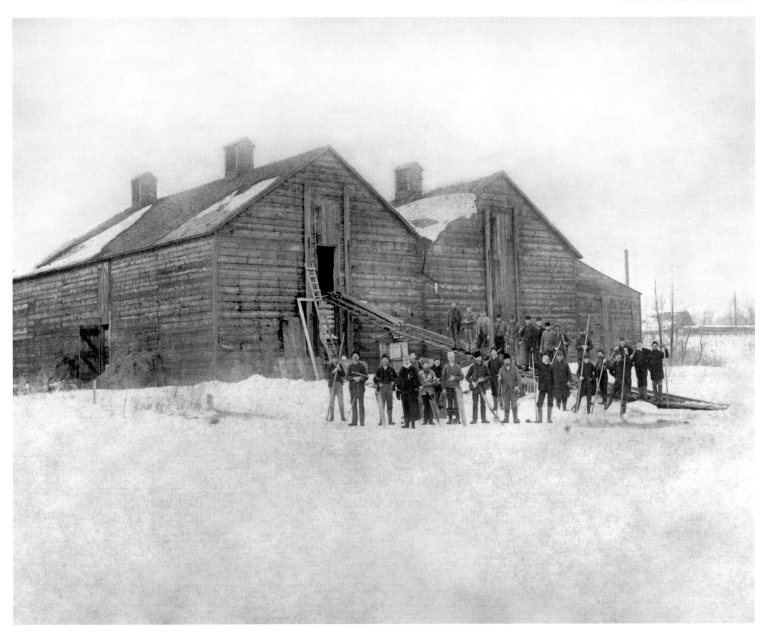

Huron Street, between Main Street and Fourth Avenue, in 1875. Cook's Hotel, on the corner of Fourth and Huron, continued as a hotel under various owners well into the twentieth century.

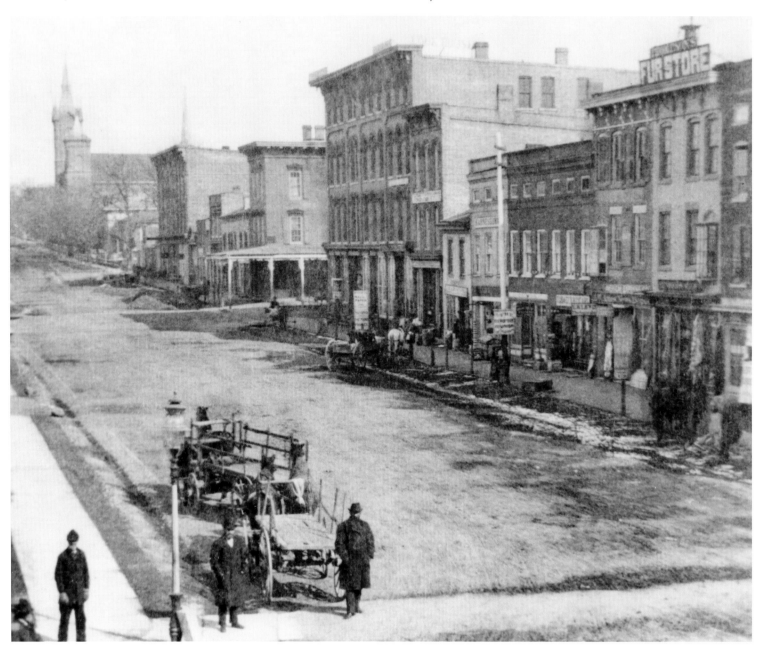

Ann Arbor Central Mills, South First Street between Liberty and Washington, ca. 1882. From the 1850s through the 1870s, this location housed various breweries—it was ideal for its proximity to the cool waters of Allen Creek, as well as to the roads leading out of Ann Arbor. In 1882, the building was purchased by the Ann Arbor Central Mills, a successful flour mill well into the twentieth century. Around 1900 the clapboard building shown here was replaced with a brick building, which still stands today.

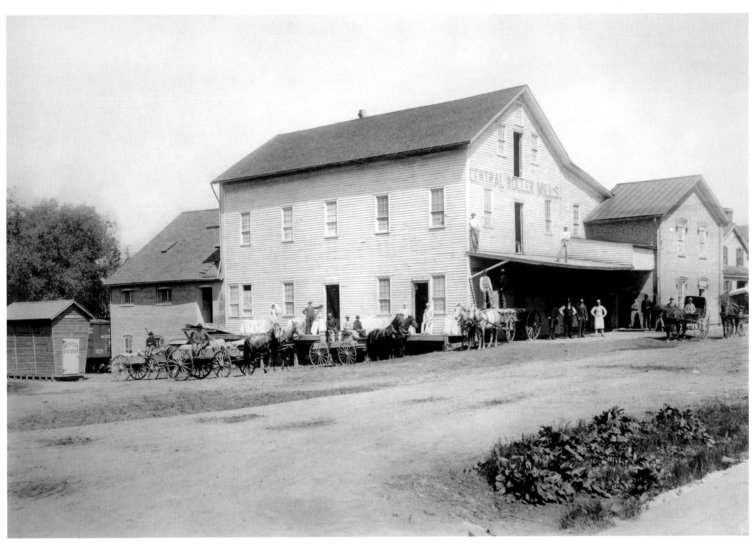

A skating party made up of men and boys poses with their dog. Skating on the Huron River and on local ponds was a popular cold-weather activity.

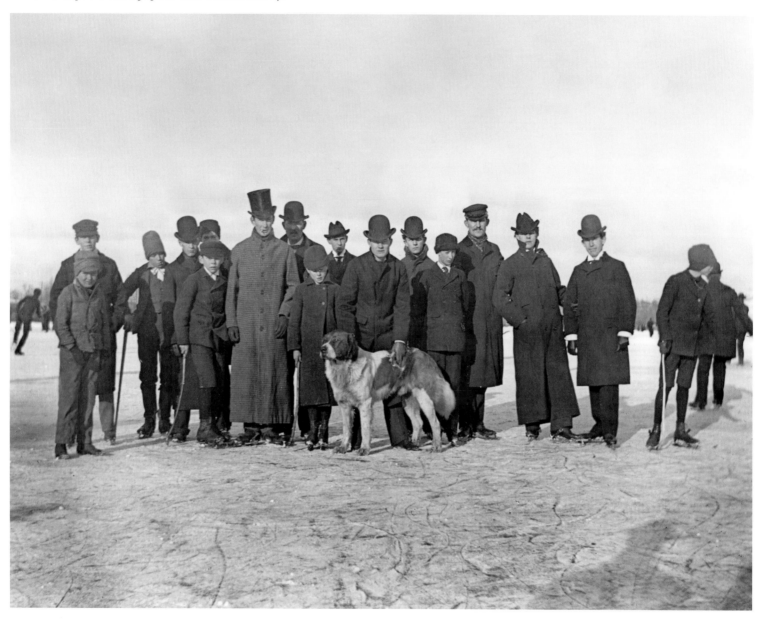

The Bank Block, at 120-124 South Main, and the northwest corner of Main and Washington, in 1876. In 1867 Philip Bach and a group of investors built this elaborate structure to house their new bank, the First National. Bach's own dry goods store was also located here, on the corner. This building would continue to house a dry goods store (under various names and owners) for more than 120 years.

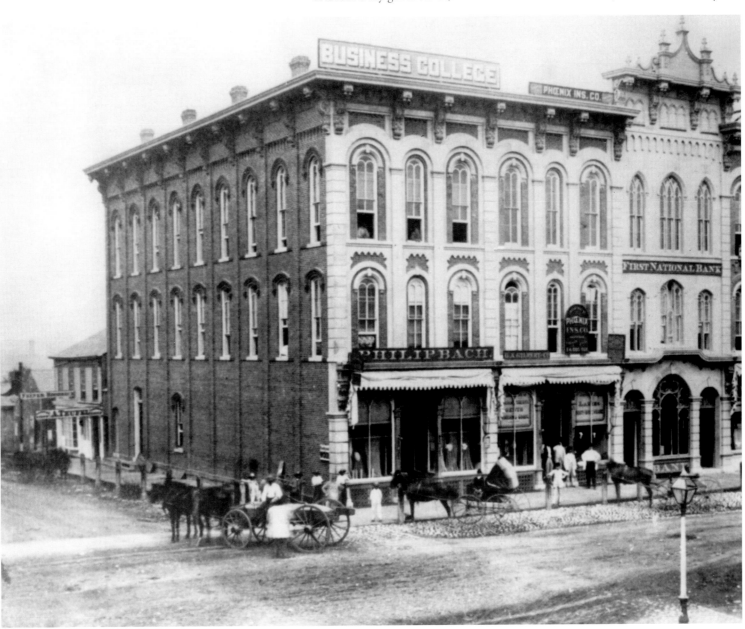

The Germania Club, ca. 1885. By 1880, German Americans made up nearly 50 percent of Ann Arbor's total population, forming many social organizations. This club often held meetings on the top floor of Michael Staebler's Germania Hotel.

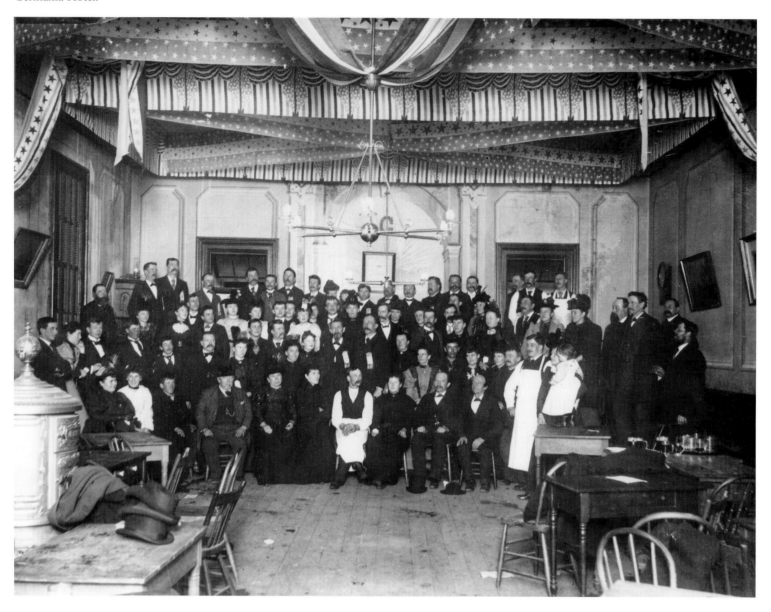

The view from University Hall, facing north, ca. 1880. This image provides a glimpse of the expanding Ann Arbor skyline, with the 1866 Methodist church on State and Washington clearly visible on the left and the arched windows on Union High School (later Ann Arbor High School) toward the right. In the foreground is the Law building.

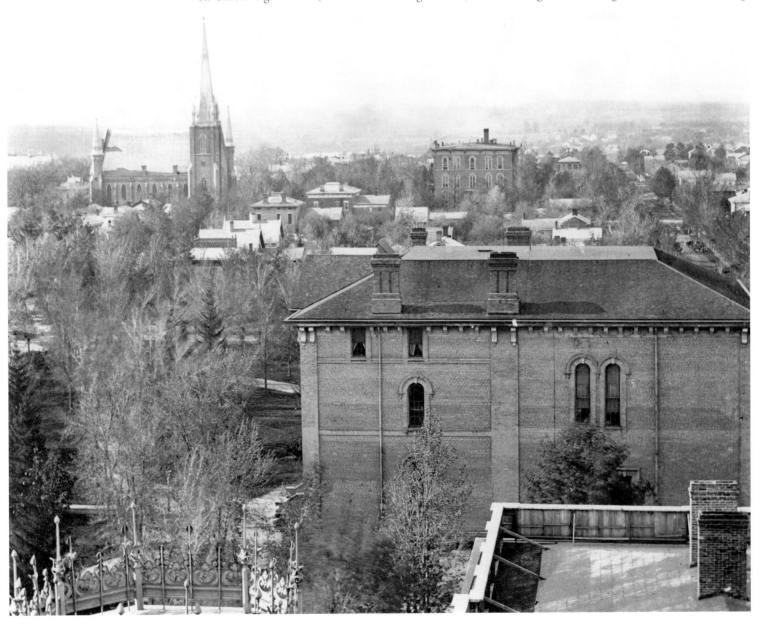

The heating plant for the University of Michigan, ca. 1883-84. This plant, located where the Randall Laboratory Building is today, provided heat for the Engineering Building, the Engineering shops, and the Physics Laboratory. It was demolished in 1894 to make way for the university's first central heating plant, which was built on the same location.

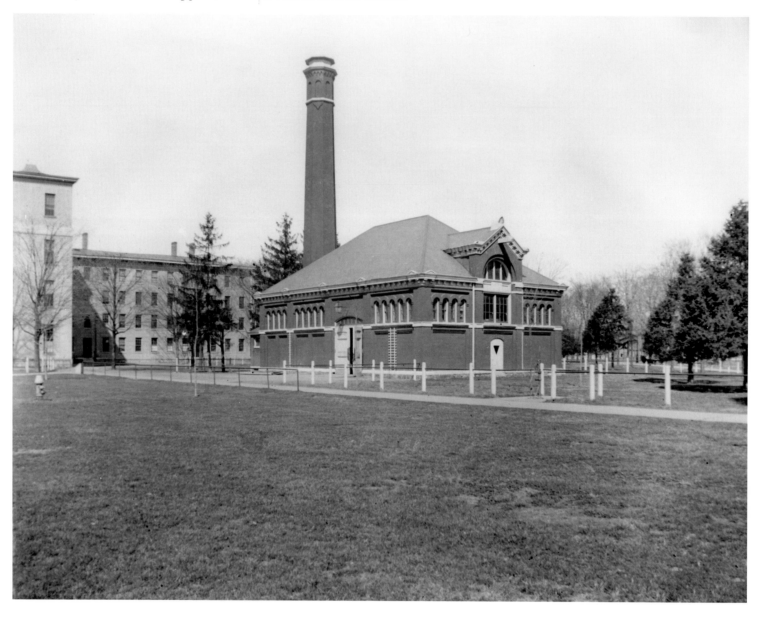

A view of State Street from North University, ca. 1880. Here are the beginnings of the development of the commercial area on State Street: Sheehan & Co.'s bookstore is located at center, and a building advertising a skating rink is to its left.

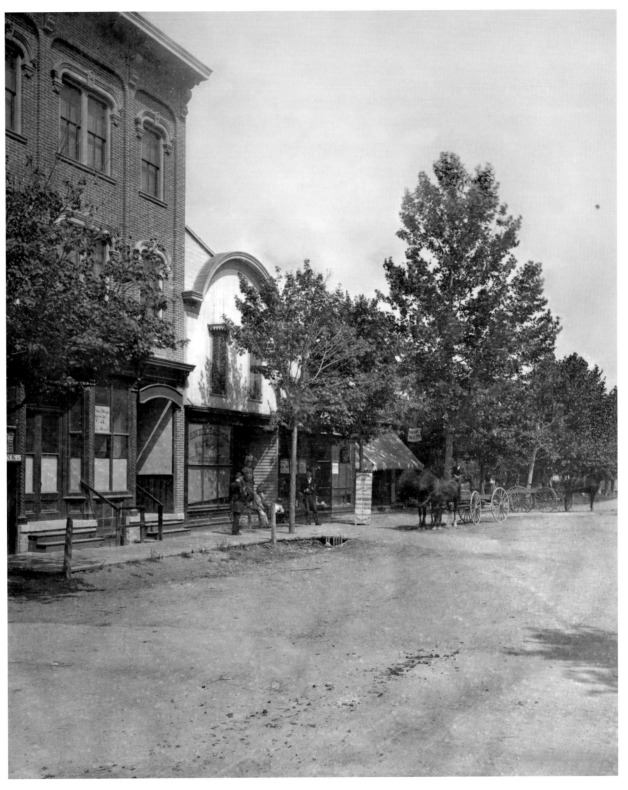

The Germania Hotel and Heinzman & Son's Harness Shop, at 117-123 West Washington, ca. 1885-90. Michael Staebler was a German immigrant who moved to Ann Arbor in 1885 and built the Germania Hotel, eventually renaming it the American Hotel. Staebler sold coal from his storefront on the right, later selling bicycles out of the same shop. He was also the first in town to sell automobiles, in 1900.

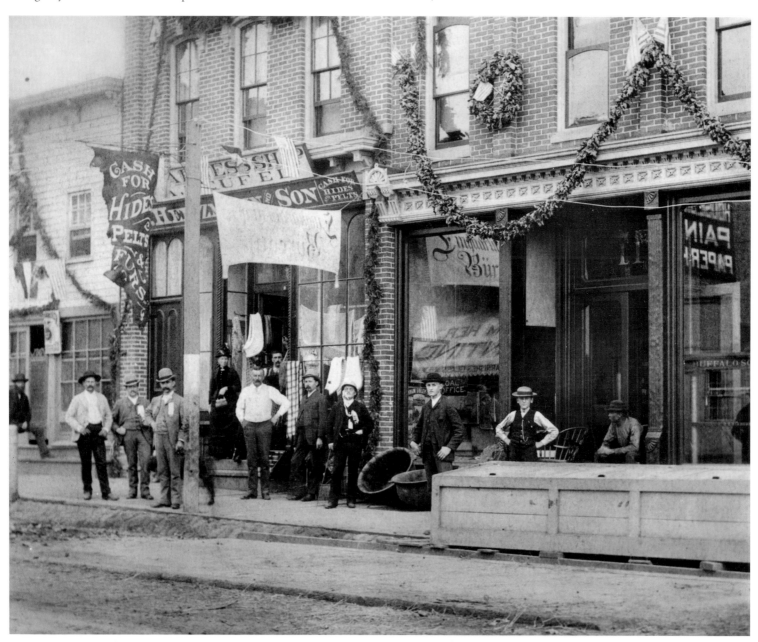

Union High School, at the northeast corner of State and Huron. The school was founded in 1856; at the time, the building was the finest in town, featuring a 700-person assembly hall. It was soon renamed Ann Arbor High School, and as the only public secondary school in the city, attracted students not only from the surrounding areas but also from farther away. The building accumulated many additions over the years, but burned down in a fire on New Year's Eve 1904. In 1907, a new building was erected, later becoming the University of Michigan's Frieze building (recently demolished).

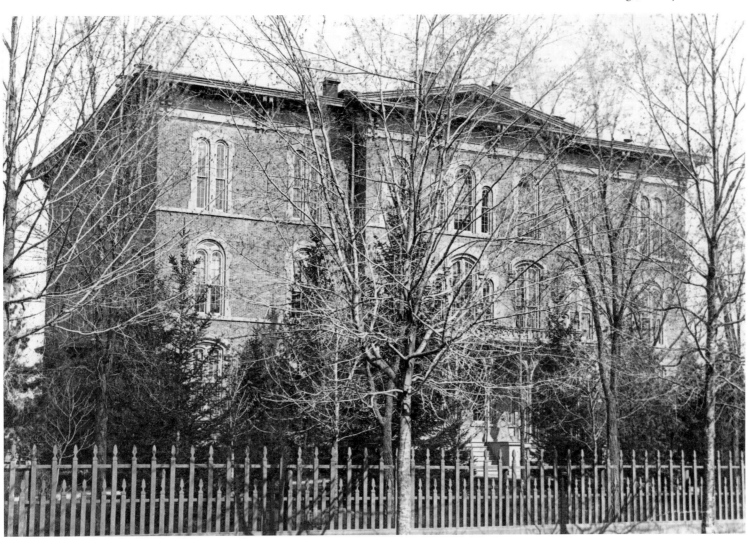

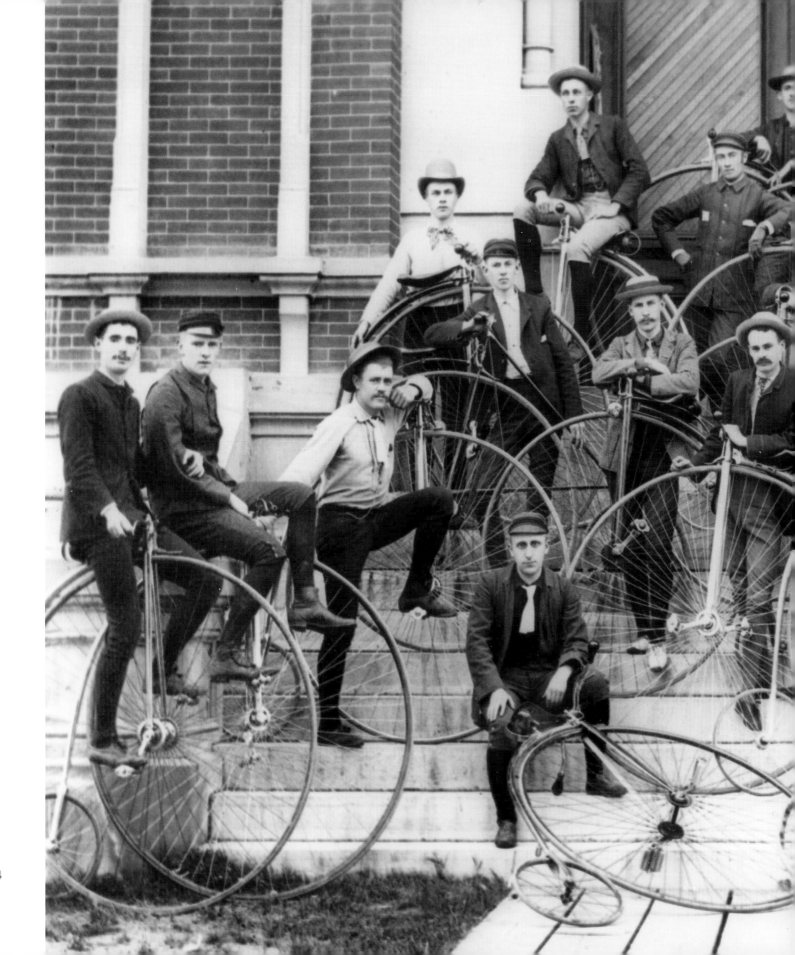

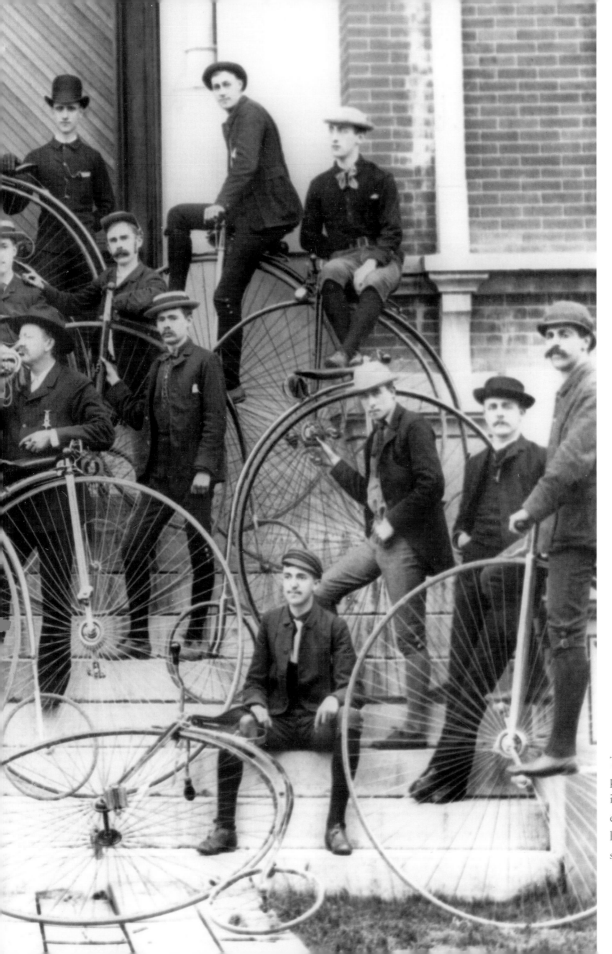

The Men's Bicycle Club poses with penny-farthings on the courthouse steps in 1887. Junius Beal, publisher and editor of the *Ann Arbor Courier* and later a University of Michigan regent, straddles his penny-farthing at far-right.

The Bach & Abel Dry Goods Store, at the corner of Main and Washington streets, in 1886. Shown here are the employees of Bach & Abel, as well as some of their merchandise, which has been displayed on the plank sidewalk. Philip Bach himself can be seen here on the right, and his partner, Eugene Abel, is the gentleman standing fourth from left. In 1895, Bach's store was purchased by Bruno St. James, whose bookkeeper, Bertha Muehlig, later owned and ran the dry goods business here from 1911 until her death in 1955.

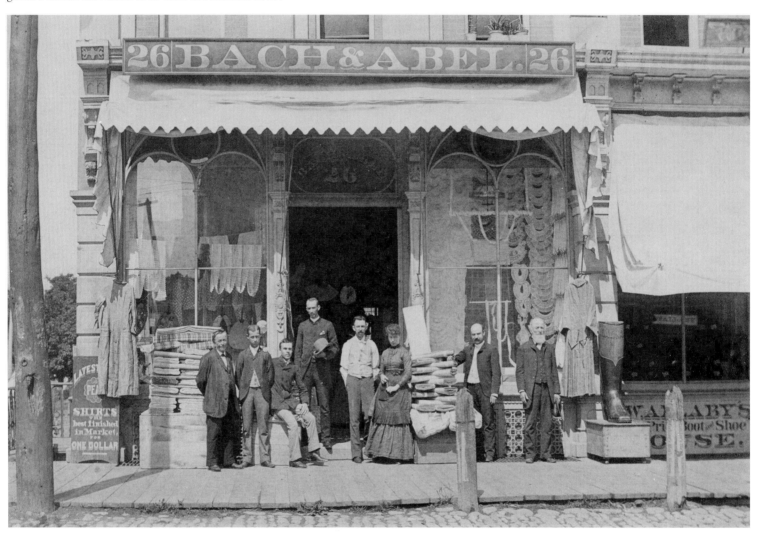

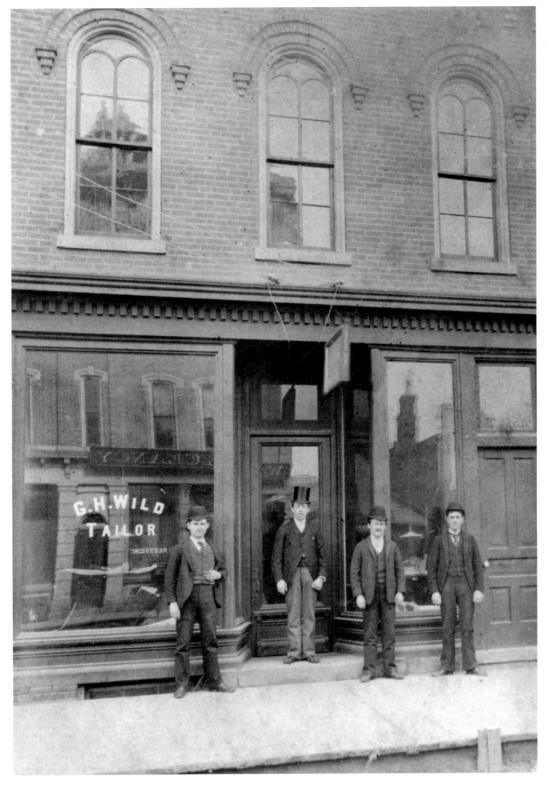

G. H. Wild's Tailor Shop, at 108 E. Washington, ca. 1890s. Gottlieb H. Wild operated his tailor shop here at the end of the nineteenth century, advertising himself as "the leading tailor for fine dress suits" in the 1894 City Directory.

Second Baptist Church, at 216 Beakes Street at N. Fourth Avenue, ca. 1890s. The church was one of two prominent black congregations in Ann Arbor to erect new structures in the 1890s. The building still stands (used today as a preschool), but the congregation has relocated to Red Oak Road.

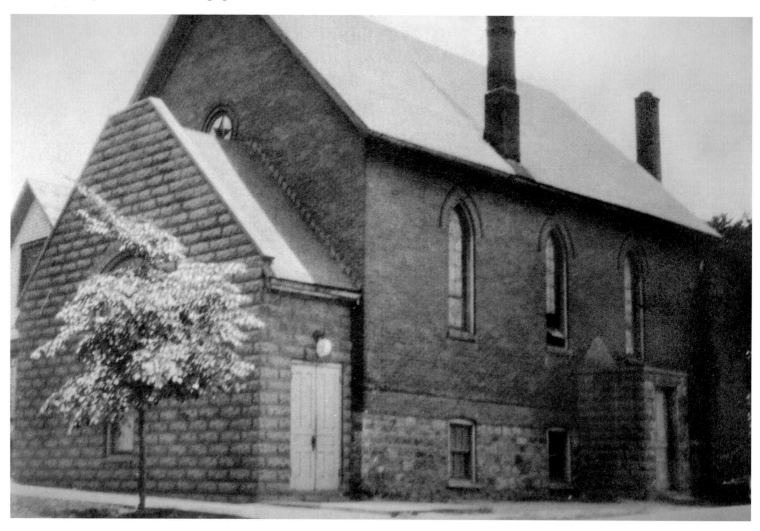

State Street at William, facing north, in 1892. In 1890 trolley service was introduced for travel between the university, downtown, and the train depot. The trolley tracks are visible in the foreground.

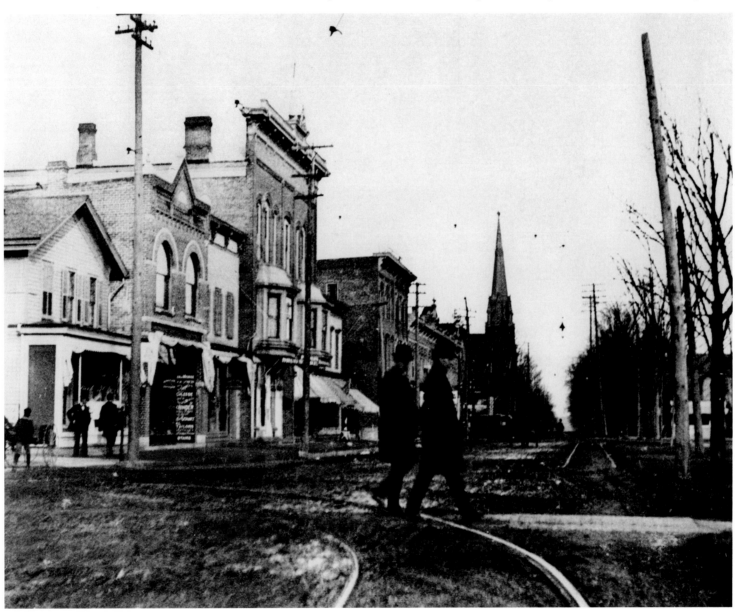

A gentleman crosses Main Street, sometime after 1890. The sign for public baths on the west side of the street indicates that although the city had running water beginning in 1885, not all of the townspeople were able to take advantage of it right away.

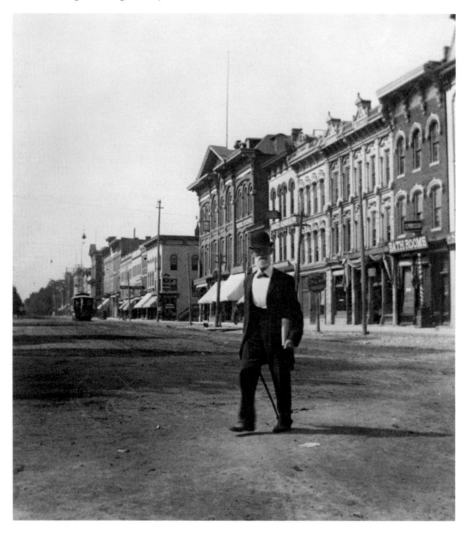

Ann Arbor newsboys in 1892. A wide array of newspapers were available for the discerning Ann Arbor reader in that year, some of which may have been hawked by youngsters like these young men in Courthouse Square. The *Ann Arbor Argus* was a Democratic rag, advertised as the oldest paper in town, and the *Ann Arbor Courier* was its Republican rival. There were also two newspapers for German immigrants and a number of other politically themed choices.

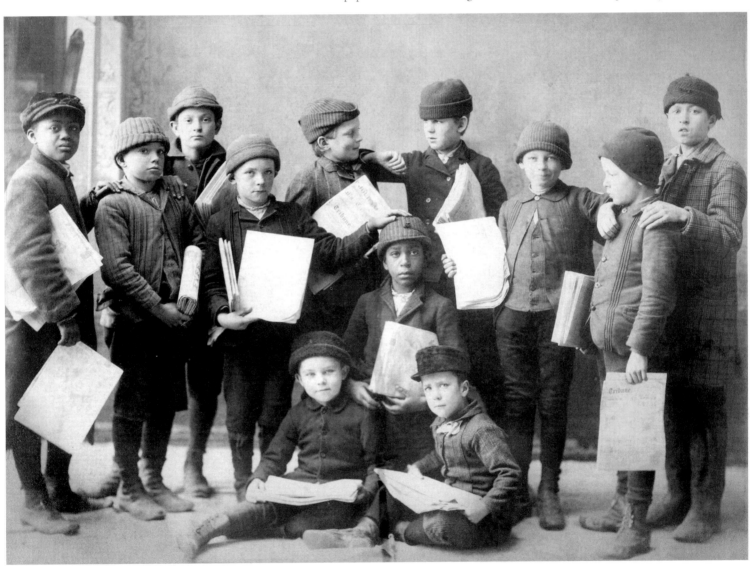

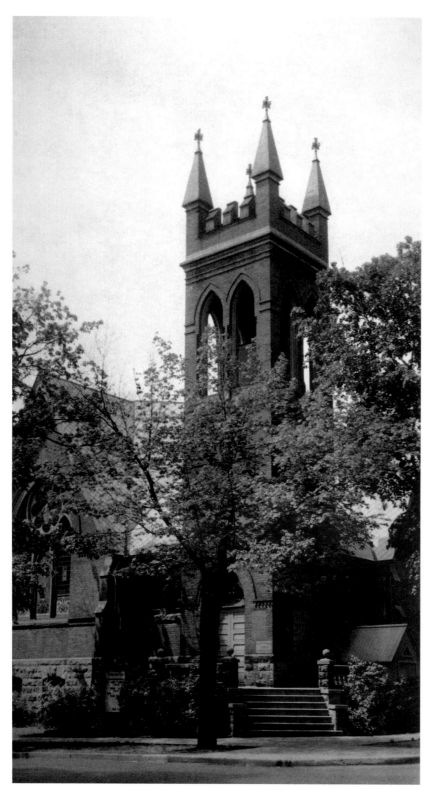

Trinity Lutheran Church, ca. 1896. The church was founded in 1893, and this structure, on the corner of William Street and 5th Avenue, was dedicated on April 5, 1896. Trinity was the first English-language Methodist church in town (all other Methodist services were given in German). When the land was sold to the YMCA in 1956 and the building demolished, the congregation moved to their current location on West Stadium Boulevard.

Blaich Bros. Grocers, at 219 South University, ca. 1899. George Blaich stands in the doorway. Blaich Bros. sold not only produce and other grocery items, but also gloves and gas lamps, as seen in the window.

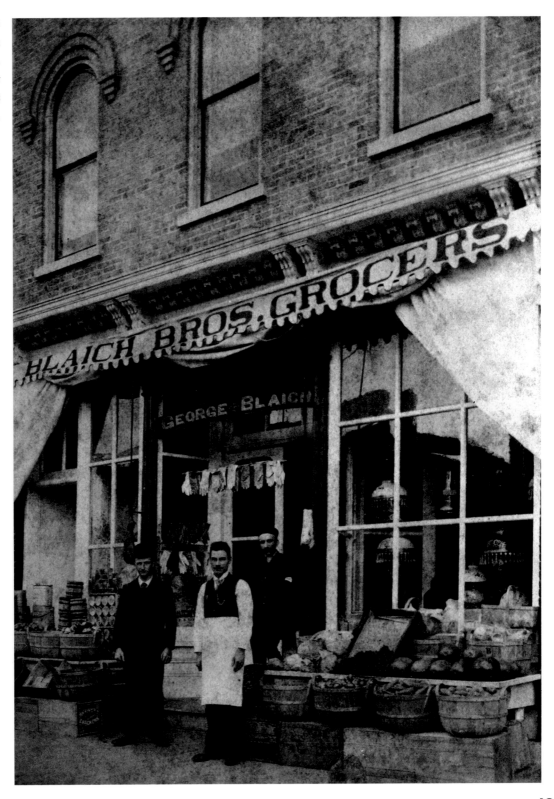

A German-American Day parade, facing east on Liberty Street, ca. 1890s. The building that housed Walker & Company's Ann Arbor Carriage Works, on the south side of the street, was built in 1886. It still stands today, home to the Ann Arbor Art Center.

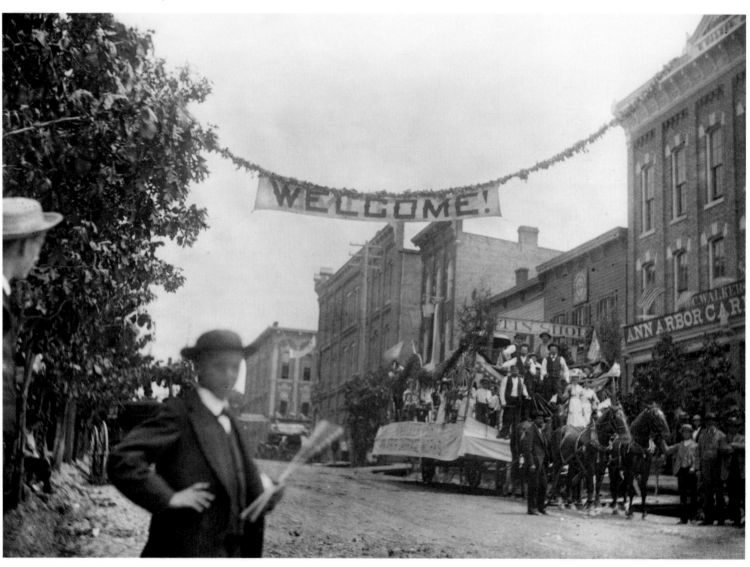

Organized in 1885 and shown here around 1894 is the all-male German singing society Lyra Gesang Verein, with mascot Elsa Kempf. Reuben Kempf (in dark suit) was the group's conductor for decades. The Kempf's house at 312 South Division Street was turned into a city museum in 1970, and the banner seen behind the group now hangs there.

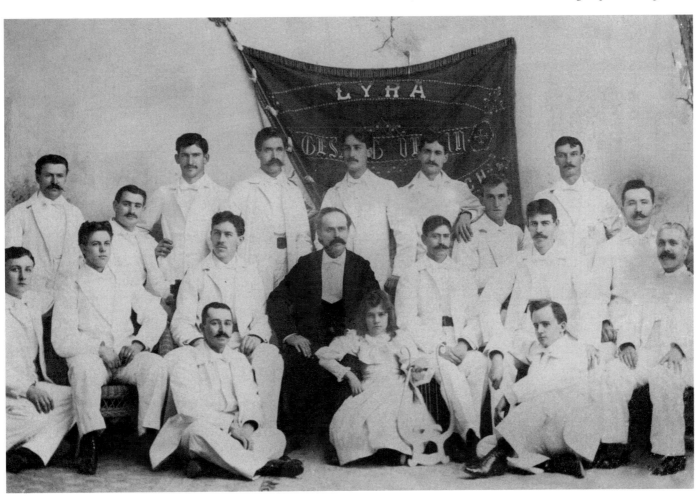

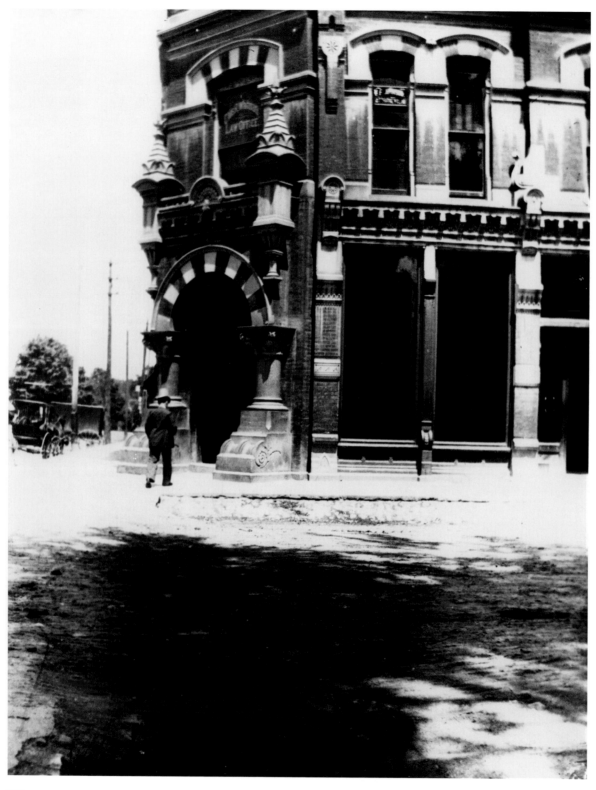

The Main Post Office, at the northeast corner of Main and Ann streets. Also known as the Beal Block, this building was constructed in 1882 by publisher Rice Beal. It served as the post office from 1882 to 1909, and was a local gathering place for townspeople, who retrieved their own mail here before home delivery began in 1886. The building was demolished in 1935.

The scene on State Street, sometime in 1893. George Wahr's bookstore at 316 S. State Street advertises textbooks at the lowest prices.

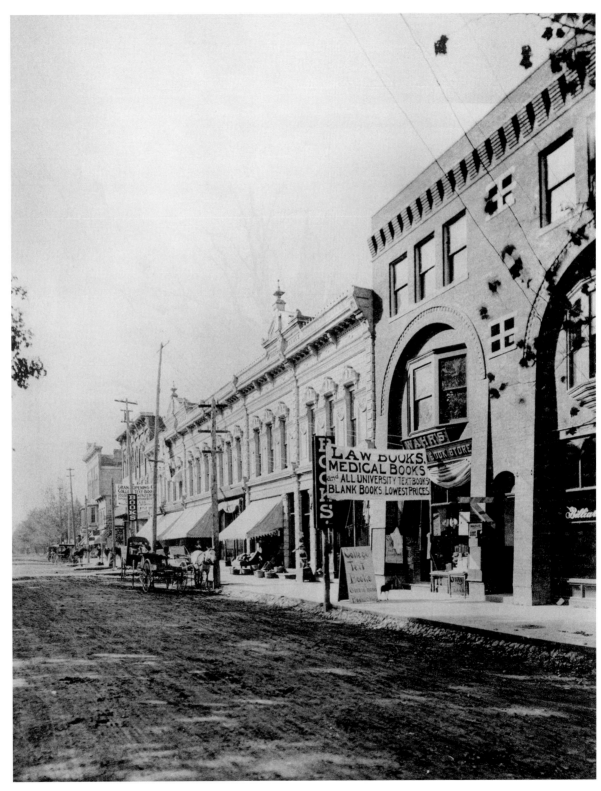

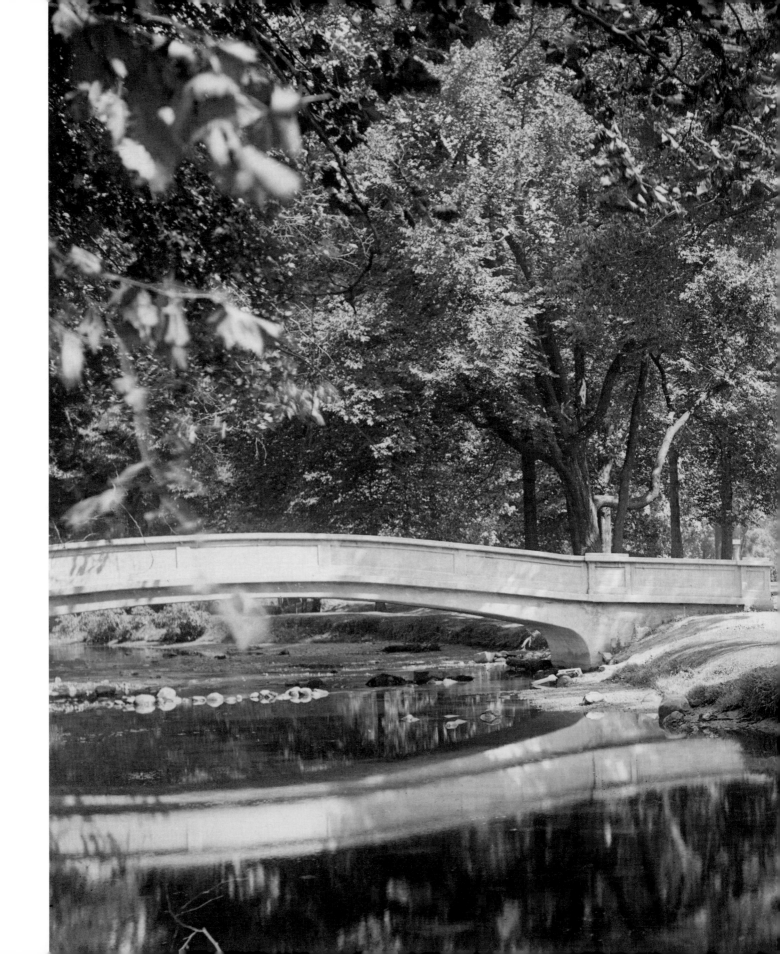

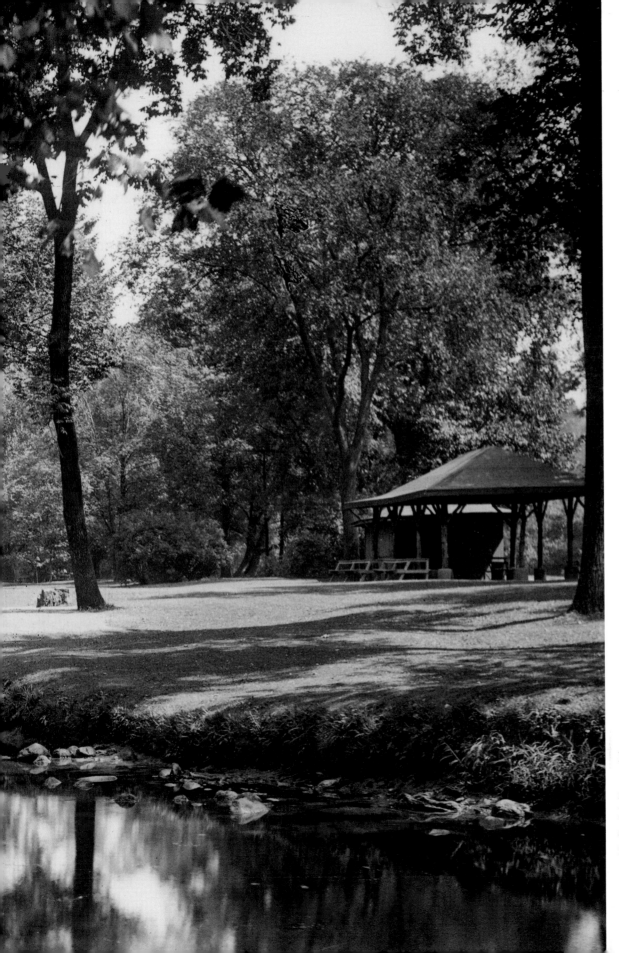

Island Park was established in the 1890s as one of Ann Arbor's first real parks. Public events, such as the Fourth of July concert given here annually by Otto's Band, added to its immense popularity.

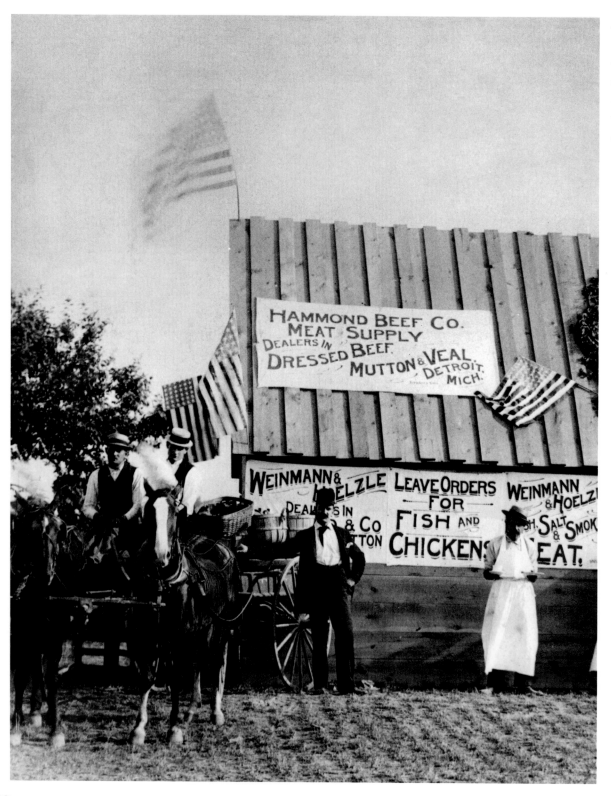

A Weinmann & Hoelzle parade float. Like most Americans, the citizens of Ann Arbor loved a parade, and parades provided an excellent opportunity for local businesses to advertise their goods.

Postal Telegraph Cable Co. operators in the Cornwell (Hamilton)
Building at East Huron and North Fourth, in the mid 1890s. This was
one of many telegraph offices that once faced Courthouse Square.

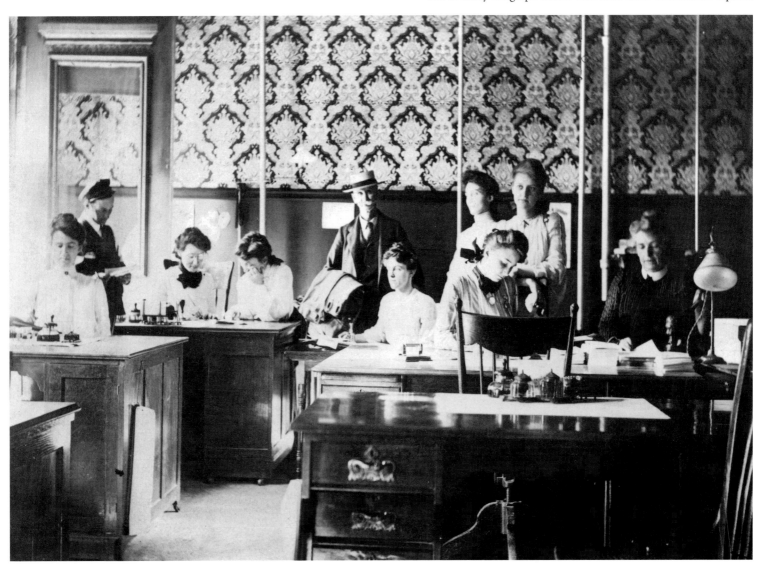

In 1881, Mack & Co.'s department store was the first local business to replace wooden sidewalks with stone slabs. As other stores and then residents followed suit, the demand for marble increased. Seen here are marble slabs being offloaded from the railroad, sometime after 1890.

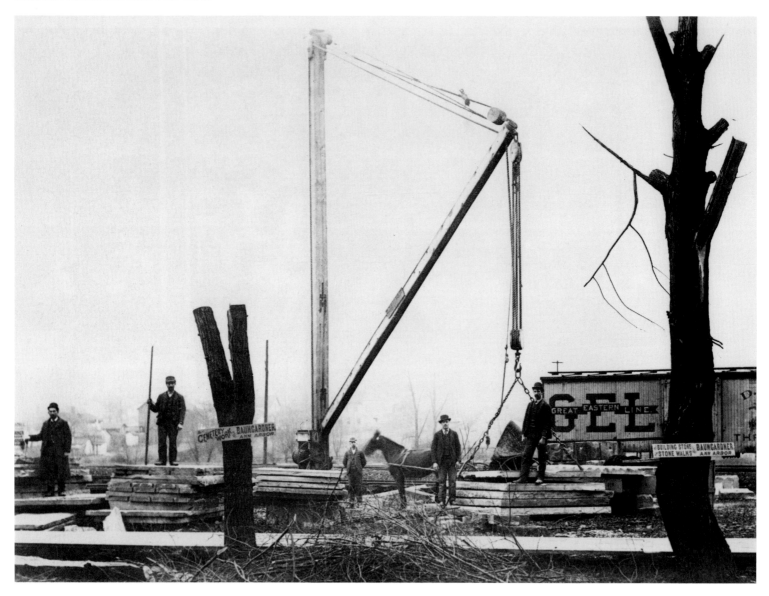

Wahr & Miller, at 218 S. Main Street, ca. 1899. This shoe store advertises fall and winter styles, but to the modern eye, the styles displayed in the window look very similar.

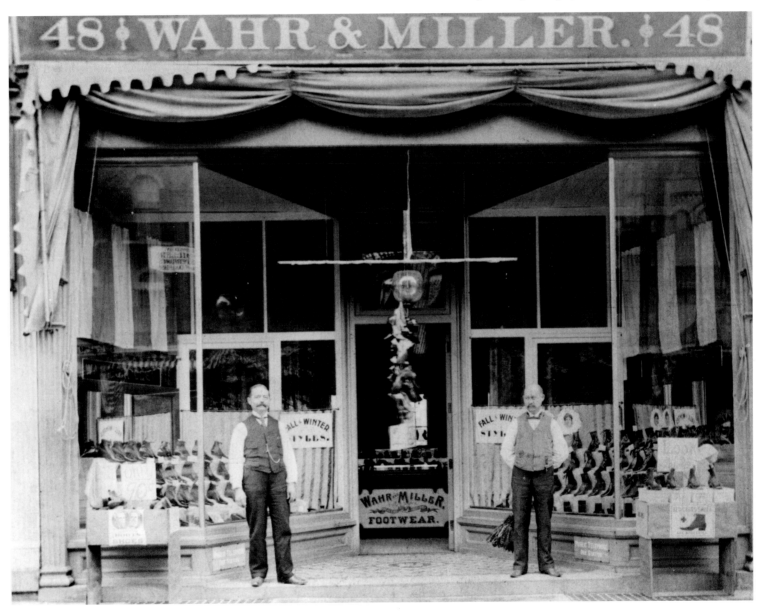

Fire breaks out at Mack & Company, on the southwest corner of Main and Liberty, on May 15, 1899. The furniture department was seriously damaged. The building was renovated and still stands at this corner, but Mack's moved across the street. It remained there, at the northwest corner of Main and Liberty, until it finally closed in 1940. By that time, Mack's had dominated the retail scene on Main Street for about 80 years.

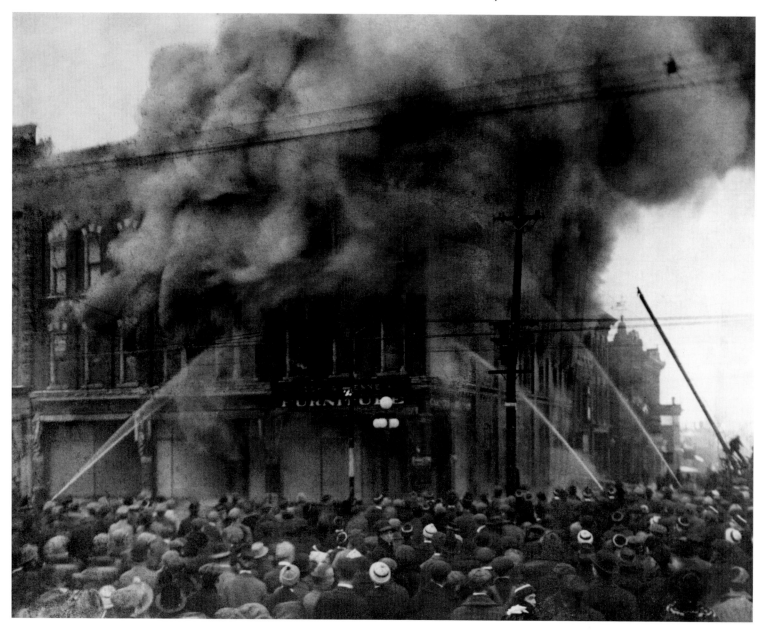

Here around the 1890s, the patriotic bunting decorating the buildings and the presence of a float suggests that a parade is in progress. Any reason to organize a parade was sufficient—from principal holidays to local developments. In 1883 the volunteer fire department celebrated their acquisition of a new hose cart with an impromptu parade through the streets, accompanied by a brass band.

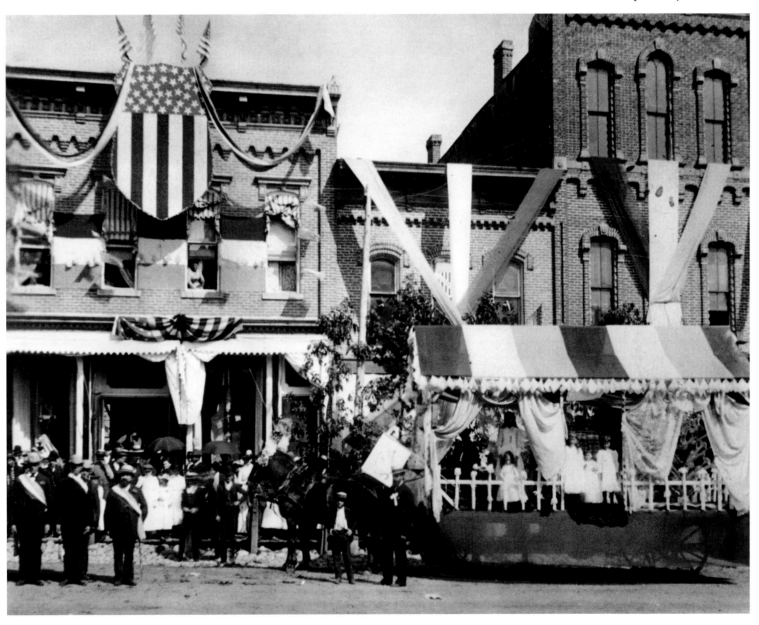

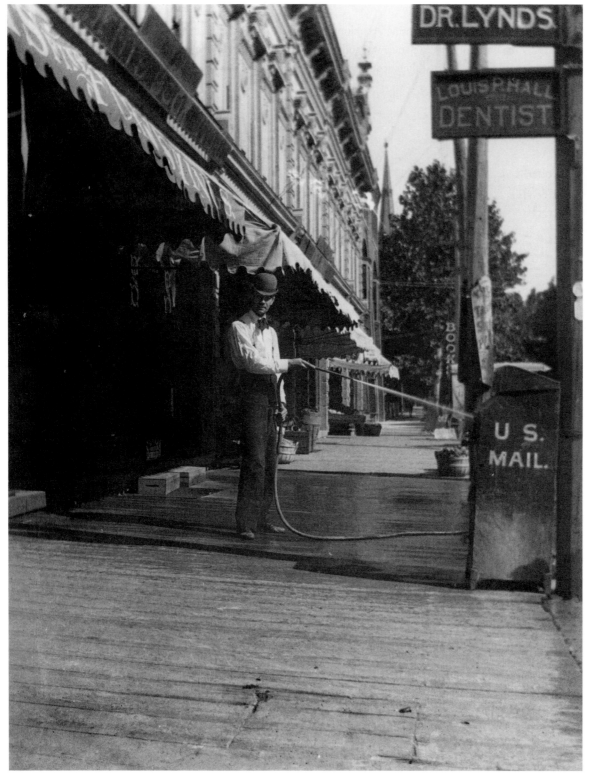

Cleaning wooden sidewalks on South State Street, before 1893. The introduction of postal collection boxes limited the need for students and townspeople living near the university to travel to the downtown post office, further hastening the commercial development of the State Street area.

North University facing east, ca. 1890s. This scene, captured on a typical winter day, illustrates one of the main frustrations that pedestrians once encountered on unpaved roads during colder weather. The muddy conditions in winter, along with the dust in summer, encouraged the Board of Public Works in 1896 to strongly recommend to the City Council that all primary business streets be paved.

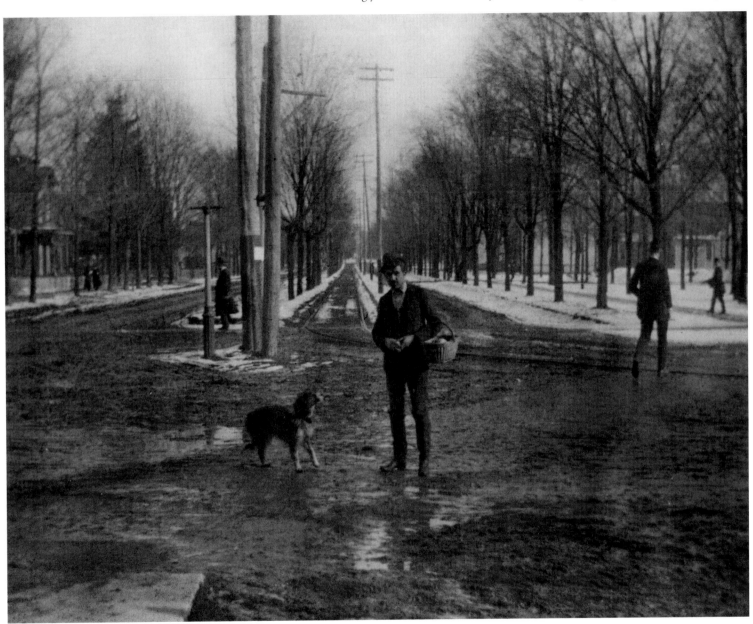

The Central Railroad Depot. Built in 1886, this train station was considered to be the finest on the Michigan Central line. The interior was as ornate as the exterior, featuring terracotta fireplaces and stained-glass windows. Travelers coming into Ann Arbor could expect to be greeted by throngs of people in the station, and by horse-drawn carriages lining the street beyond to take them to their destination. This building is now home to the Gandy Dancer restaurant.

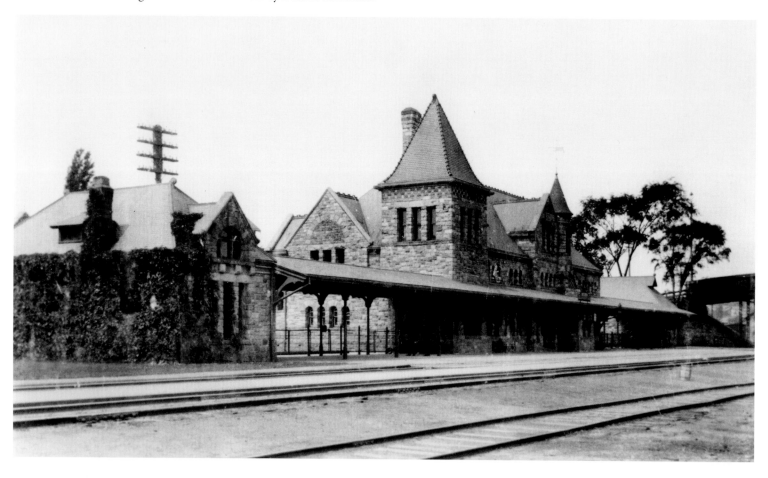

State Street, in 1892. By
this time a multitude of
bookstores lined State Street,
much as they do now.

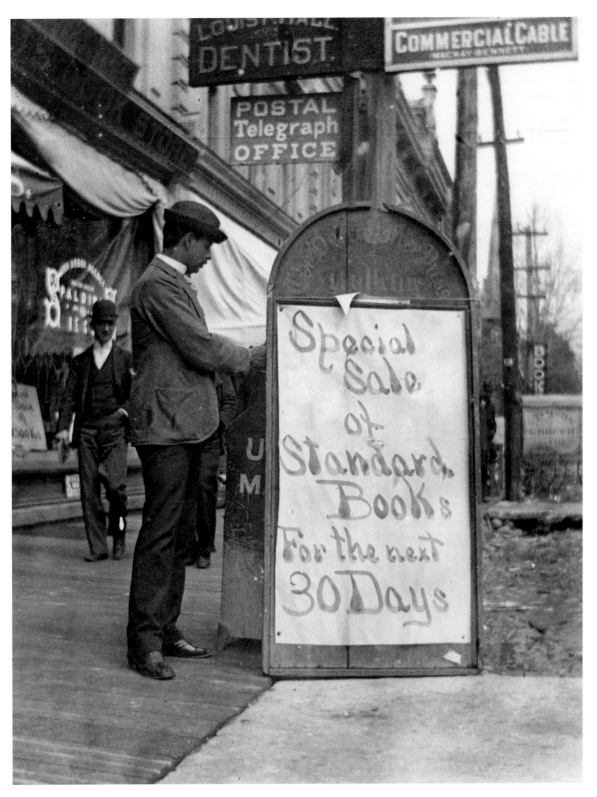

In 1898, employees of the Hutzel & Co. hardware store and plumbing firm demonstrate some new items—useful thanks to the installation of running water and a sanitary sewer system. The items on this parade float include flush toilets and claw-foot bathtubs.

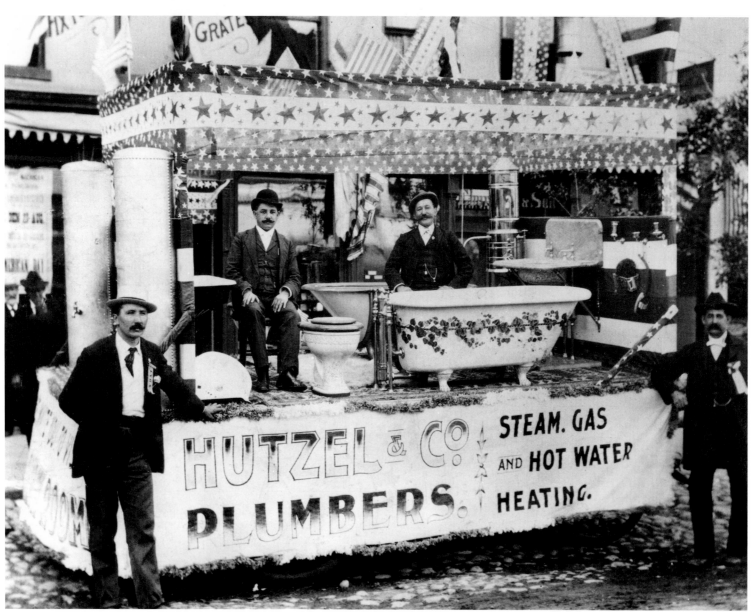

Railway passengers wait for the train to clear the Broadway Bridge, ca. 1890s.

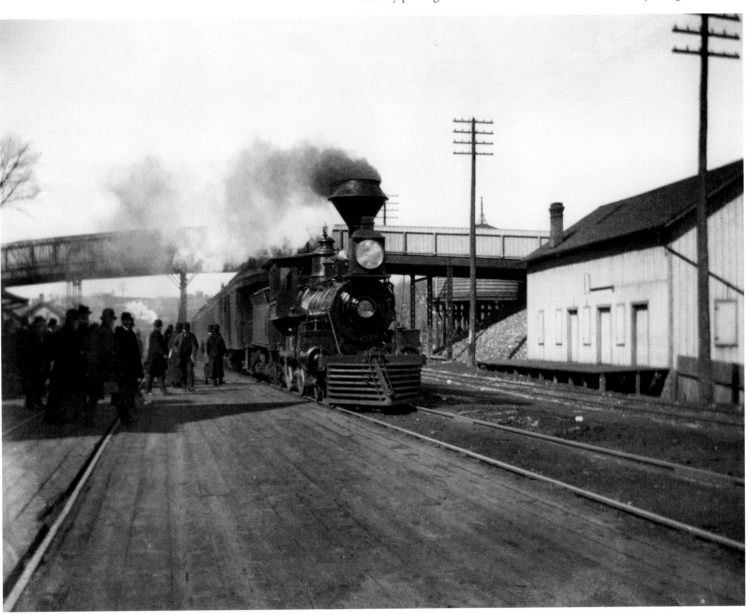

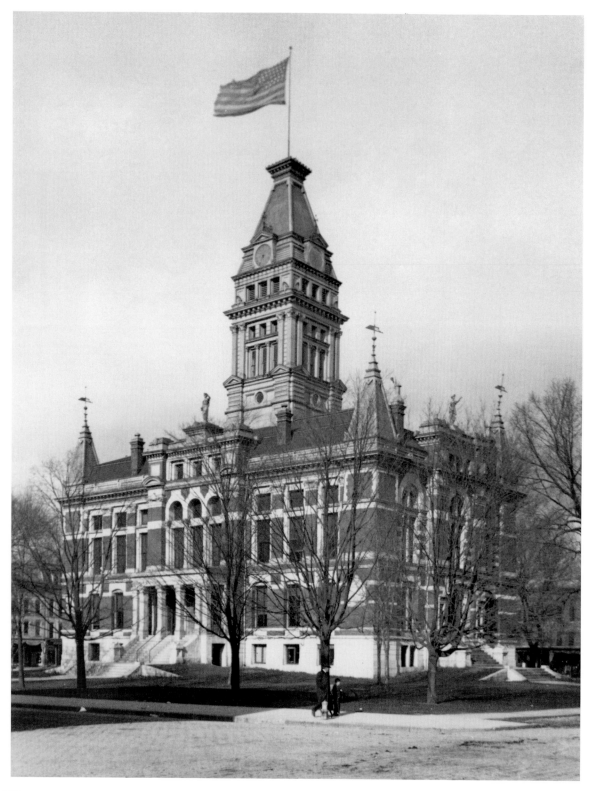

The Second Courthouse. This courthouse, beautiful though it was, was eventually replaced. The tower was removed as a fire hazard in 1948, and an entirely new courthouse was built beside it in 1957. The site of this building is now a parking lot for the newer building.

The "Diag," at the corner of State and North University, after 1890. As evidenced by the sign at the entrance to campus, the sale of University of Michigan souvenirs was already a popular commercial pursuit.

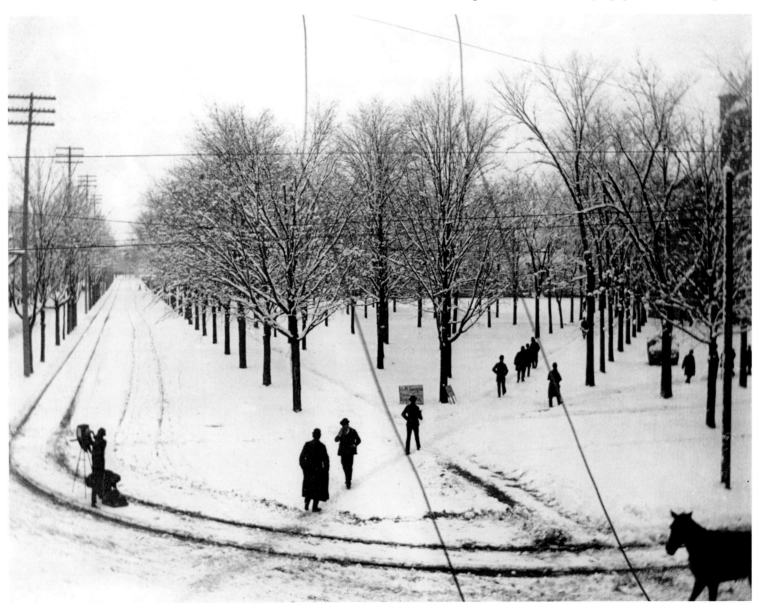

The Ann Arbor Organ Company, at the southeast corner of Main and Liberty streets, in 1893. The organs and pianos that were made in David Allmendinger's factory were sold here in his retail store.

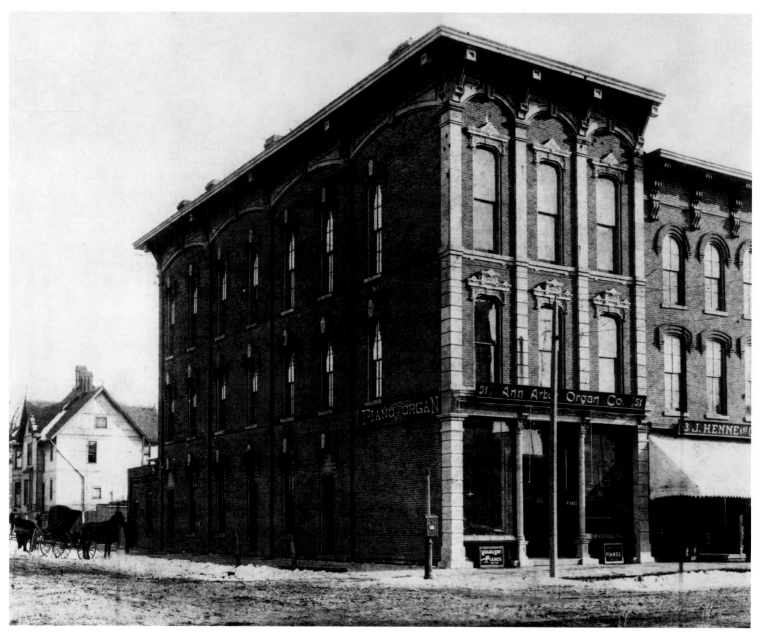

A derailment at Miller Avenue in 1893. Disasters such as fires and train derailments often brought out the whole town. Here a few curious townspeople and children approach the stranded steam engine.

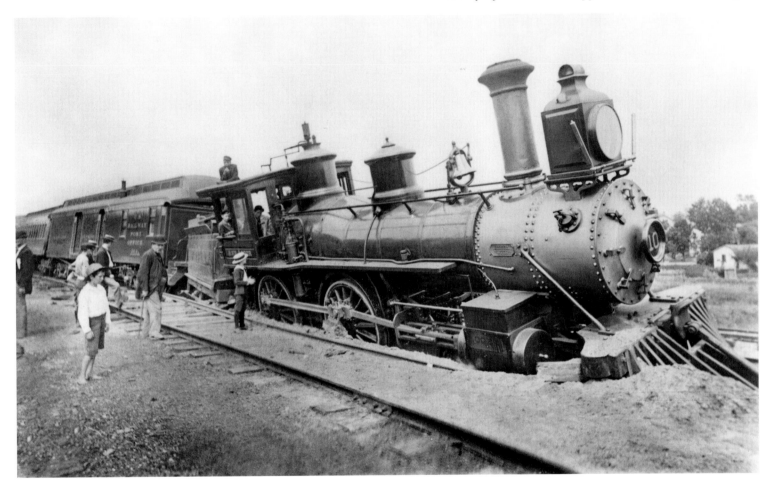

A parade on Main Street, ca. 1898-1900. For decades after its construction, the courthouse remained a focal point of the town, and any parade would necessarily pass right in front of it. On the corner of Main and Ann streets is the Main Post Office. The streets are now paved, but it is clear that just a few blocks north, Main Street remains undeveloped.

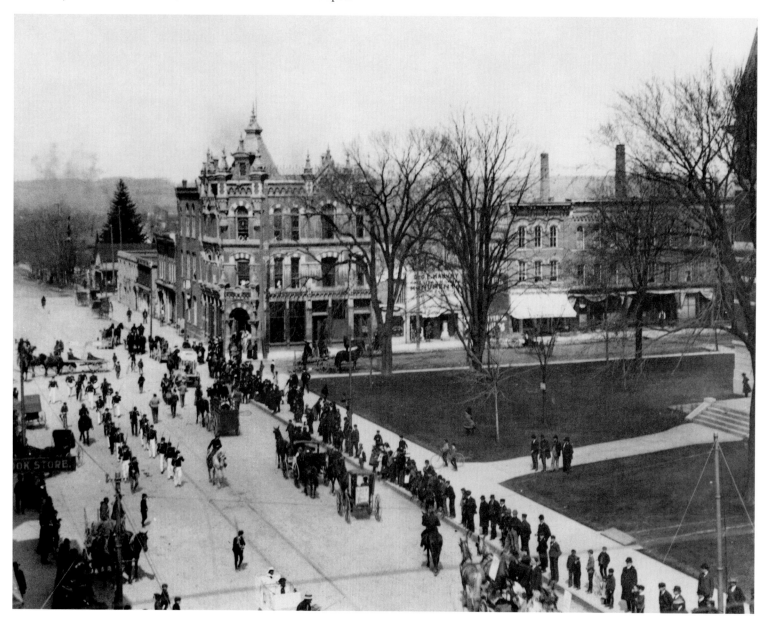

Seen here in 1895, this float, decorated with apples, has presumably stopped on its way to join a harvest-themed parade. Visible behind the float is the Buchoz Block, located at Detroit Street. On the far right is the Half Way Saloon, whose name referred to the location of the block on the trolley line, halfway between the railroad depot and downtown.

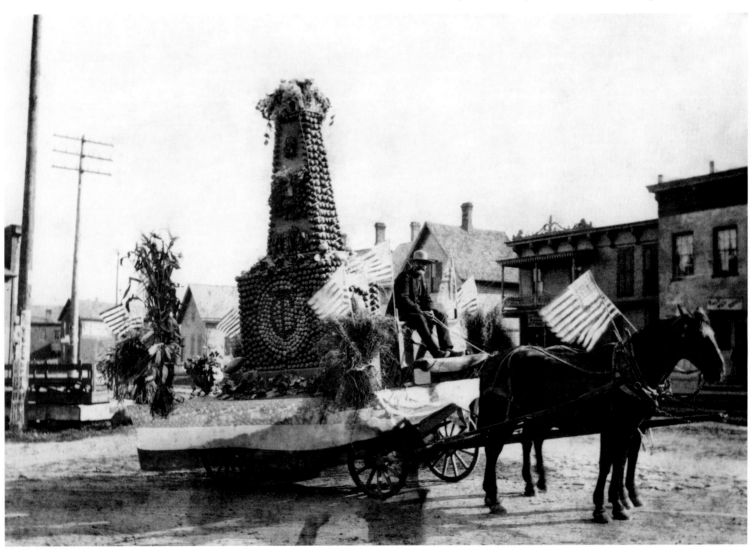

An important citizen seems to be riding in his carriage in this 1897 parade, possibly doffing his hat to the assembled crowd. A concession stand sells hot sausage and soft drinks in the background.

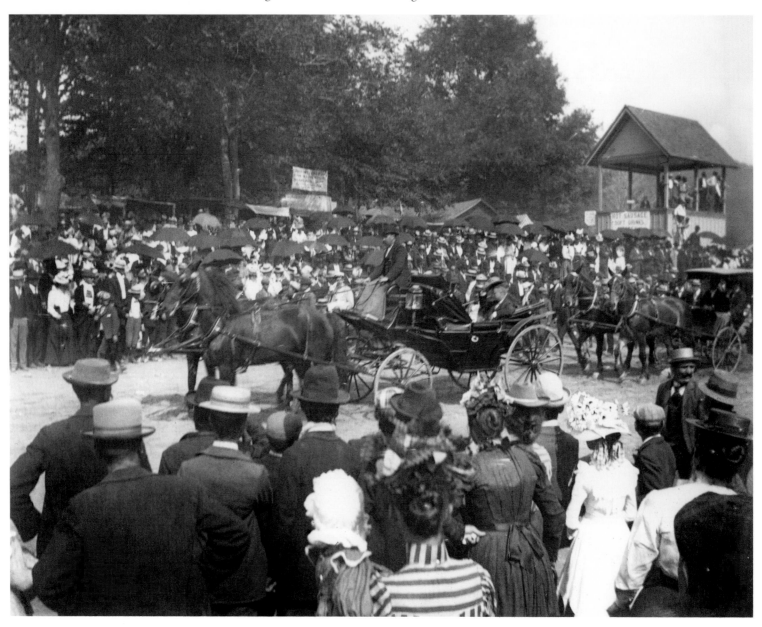

Two conductors pose in front of a Packard-Huron streetcar, ca. 1890s. Ann Arbor's streetcar line operated from 1890 until 1924, when, with much fanfare, the old cars were replaced with buses.

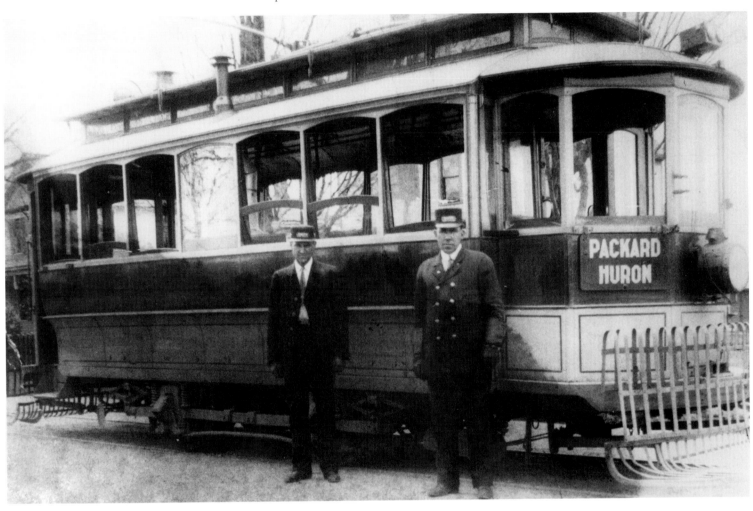

The old University Library, ca. 1890s. The first library building, built in 1883, served not only as a library, but also as an art gallery. When it was replaced with the Harlan Hatcher Library in 1920, architects chose to build around the older structure, with the result that the first library's stacks are still in use.

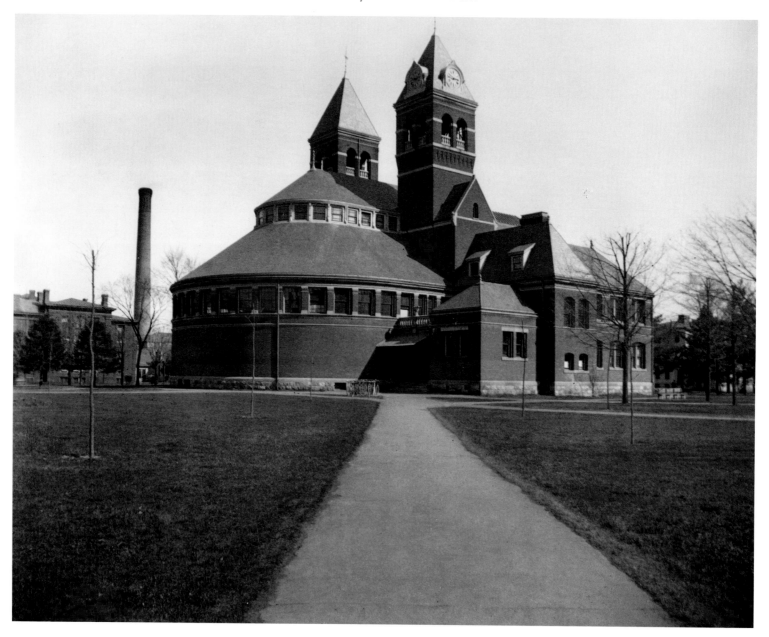

First Baptist Church, at Huron Street between Division and State, late in the nineteenth century. The First Baptist Church was founded in 1828, and spent its early years frequently changing locations. The congregation was located in Lower Town from 1832 to 1849, then on Catherine Street until 1881, when its current home (shown here) was completed.

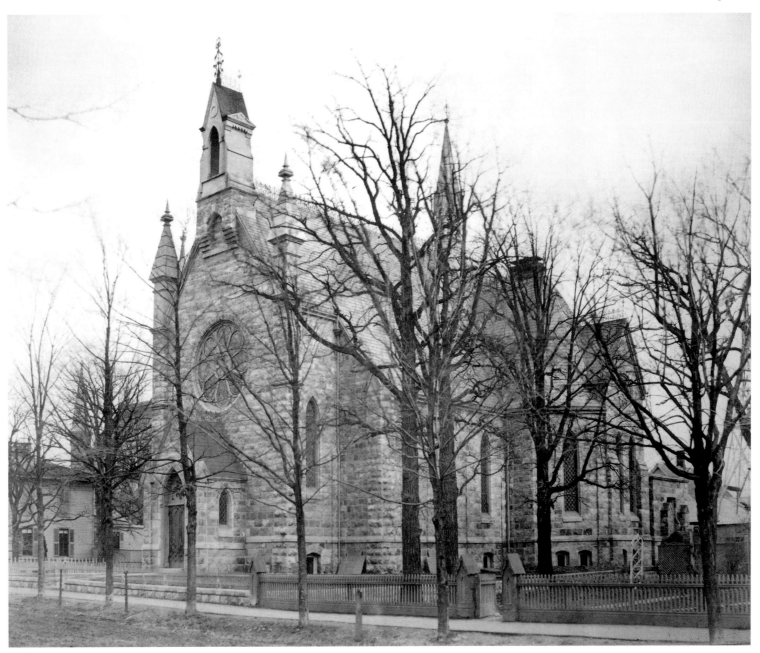

Ann Arbor's Company A, First Infantry, Michigan National Guard, 1898. The Company posed on the courthouse steps for a formal portrait before leaving for the Spanish-American War. This group of volunteer soldiers was headed for Cuba.

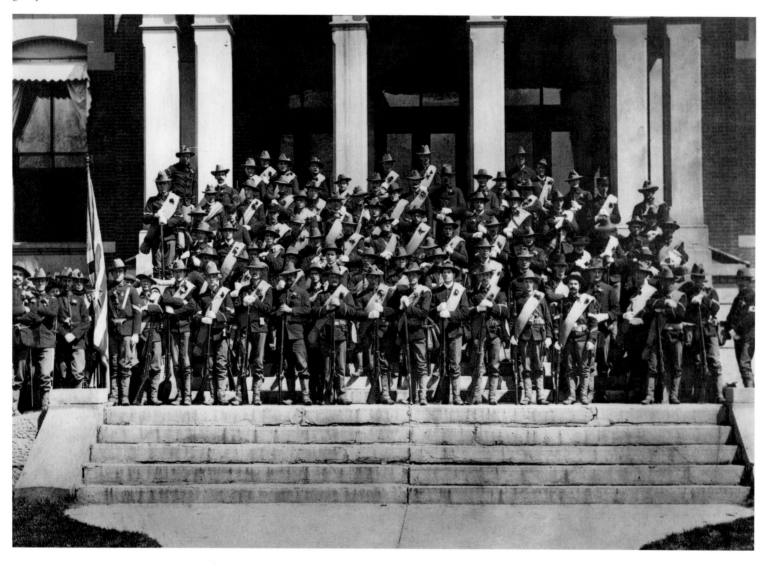

AUTOMOBILES, WAR, AND INFLUENZA

(1900–1919)

The first decade of the new century was relatively quiet for Ann Arbor. The population, at 14,500 in 1900, remained stable until 1910, when it increased again. Public services that had been established at the end of the nineteenth century became more standardized during this time. The Ann Arbor Water Company, a source of tension for its inadequate and unsafe water, was bought by the city in 1913. The same year, the Ann Arbor Civic Association sought to improve many conditions in town, setting up a Good Roads Committee, seeking better garbage collection, and encouraging a practice of milk and meat inspection for neighboring farms. The Civic Association also pursued an aggressive anti-fly crusade, arming hundreds of schoolchildren with flyswatters in an attempt to rid the city of this nuisance.

The first automobile in the city was introduced in 1900 by Michael Staebler, the owner of the American Hotel on Liberty Street. Automobiles were slow to catch on in Ann Arbor—it was not until 1910 that Mayor William Walz found it necessary to issue the first city rules for driving and parking. A sign of the changing times can be seen in the story of Walker's Livery: in 1912, Walker's was still the largest livery in town, with thirty horses. Only two years later the horses and equipment were auctioned off, and the company soon after acquired a fleet of automobiles, rechristening itself the Ann Arbor Taxicab and Transfer Company.

The arrival of World War I affected Ann Arbor in a number of direct and indirect ways. Ethnic tensions erupted, aimed at the city's large German-American population. In the fall of 1918 the Spanish influenza pandemic that swept the world also reached Ann Arbor. Students, faculty, and townspeople were urged to wear face masks, and out of the hundreds who fell ill, more than one hundred lost their lives to the disease. Also in 1918, statewide prohibition (mandated in Michigan's November 1916 election) was put into effect, closing the saloons and breweries that had long made their home in the city. Armistice finally came in November 1918, and many of the Ann Arbor men who had gone off to fight in the Great War returned home. After the war ended, Ann Arbor was poised to welcome in yet another era of growth and change.

A daring fellow staddles a telephone pole above State Street, ca. 1900. Although the first telephone exchange in Ann Arbor was established in 1881, the service was very expensive. For many years, only businesses and a limited number of wealthy townspeople could afford to have their own lines installed. In 1897, a second private company with cheaper rates established service in the area and forced down prices, making it easier for townspeople to afford telephones.

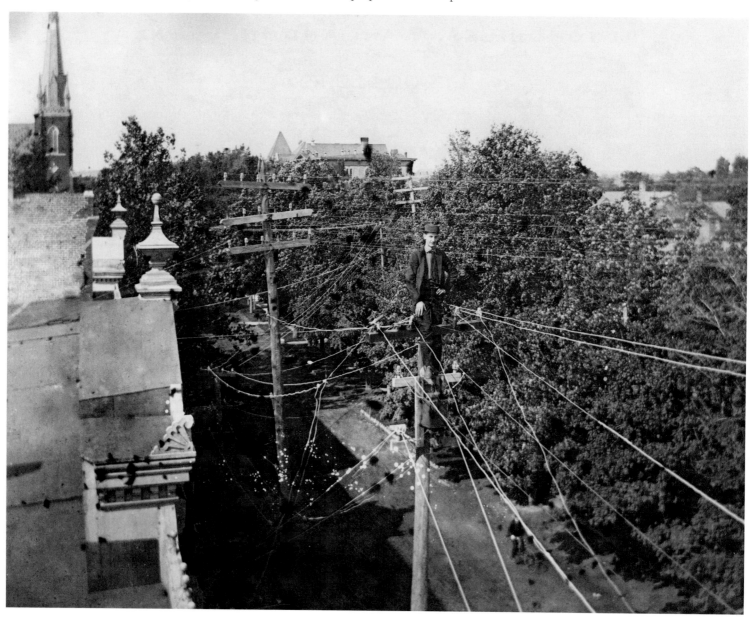

Main Street, facing north from Liberty Street, ca. 1908. In the foreground is Mack and Company, Ann Arbor's largest department store. By 1908, Main Street was fully paved (brick paving was installed in 1898), and townspeople wishing to do their shopping could travel streets that were dust-free, by trolley or horse-drawn carriage.

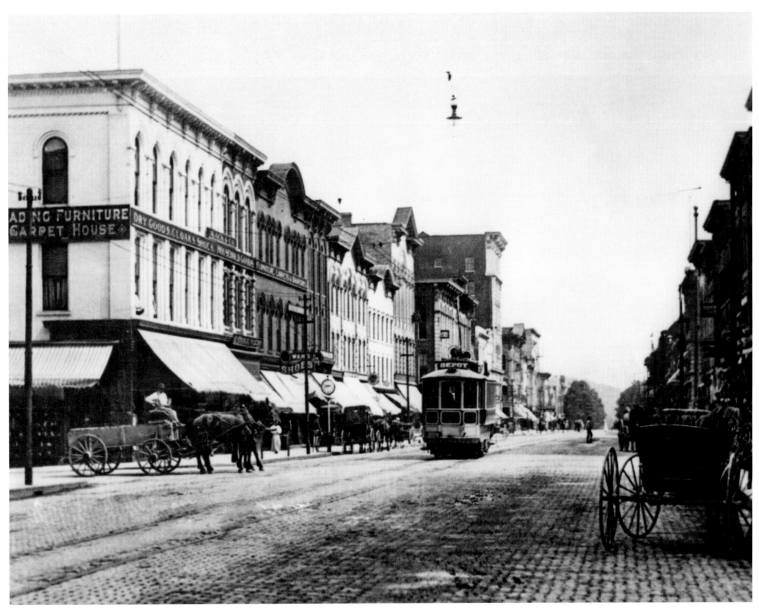

The Michigan Beef & Provision Company at 140 South State Street, in the early 1900s. Stone sidewalks had been installed by this time, but refrigeration was still many years away.

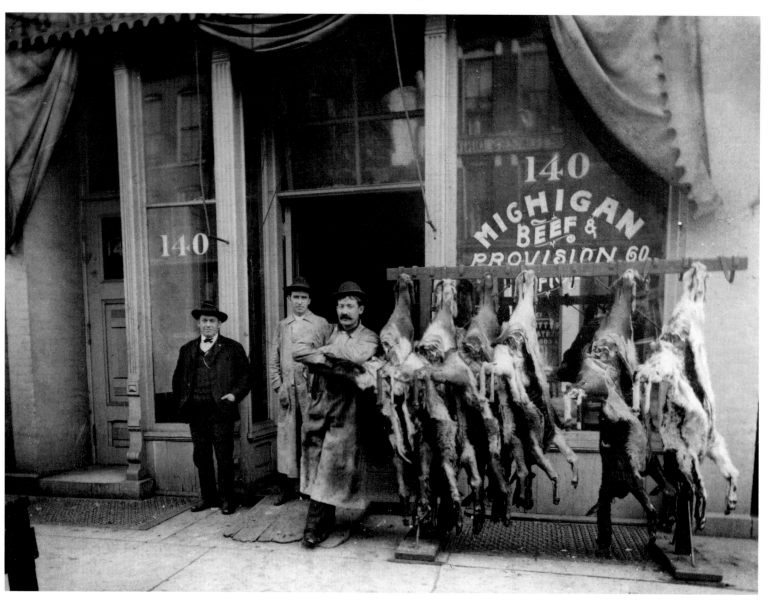

A flotilla of canoes on the Huron River, probably early 1900s. The occupants are all gazing toward the canoes at center-right, where a contest of some kind seems to be in progress.

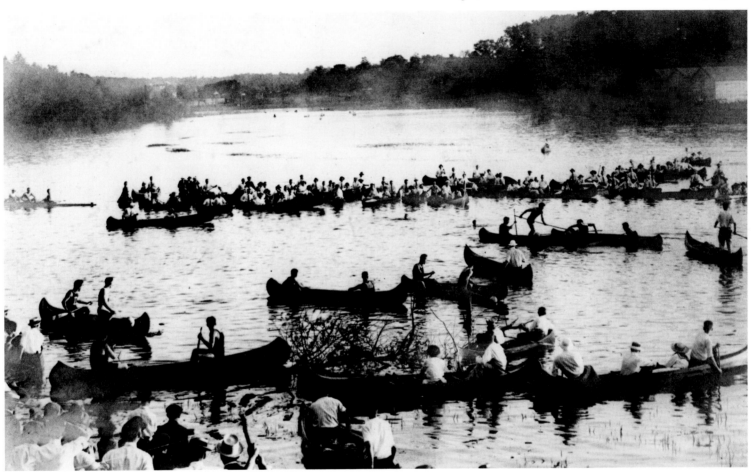

Man with a bicycle, ca. 1900. With the invention of pneumatic tires, riding a bicycle became much more comfortable, and therefore even more popular in Ann Arbor.

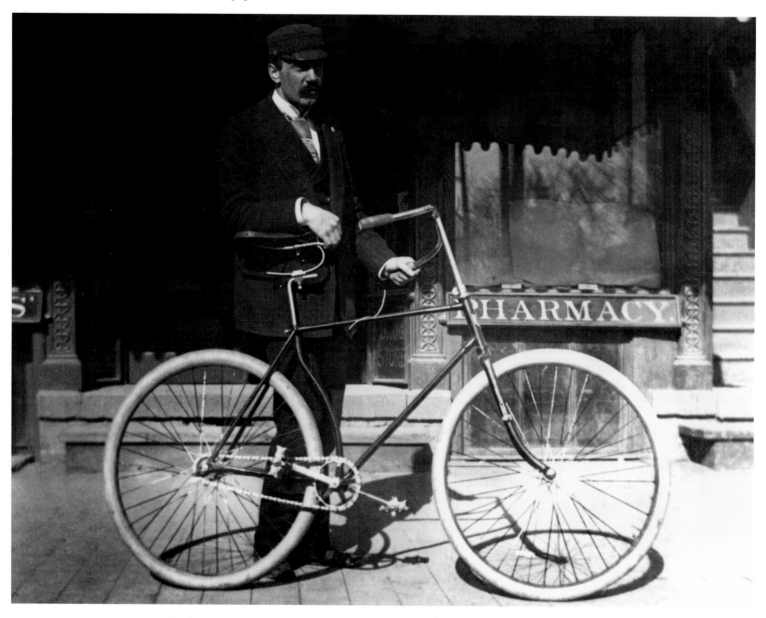

The Savings Bank Block, northwest corner of Main and Huron, ca. 1905. The Ann Arbor Savings Bank was organized in 1869, making it the third oldest bank in Ann Arbor. This building previously housed the Gregory Hotel.

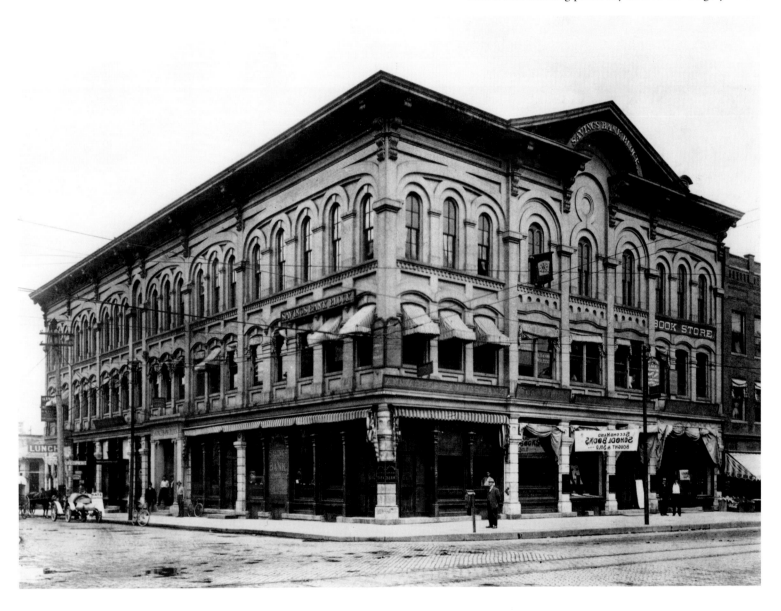

Around 1910, this bar featured not only electric light fixtures, but also an electric ceiling fan.

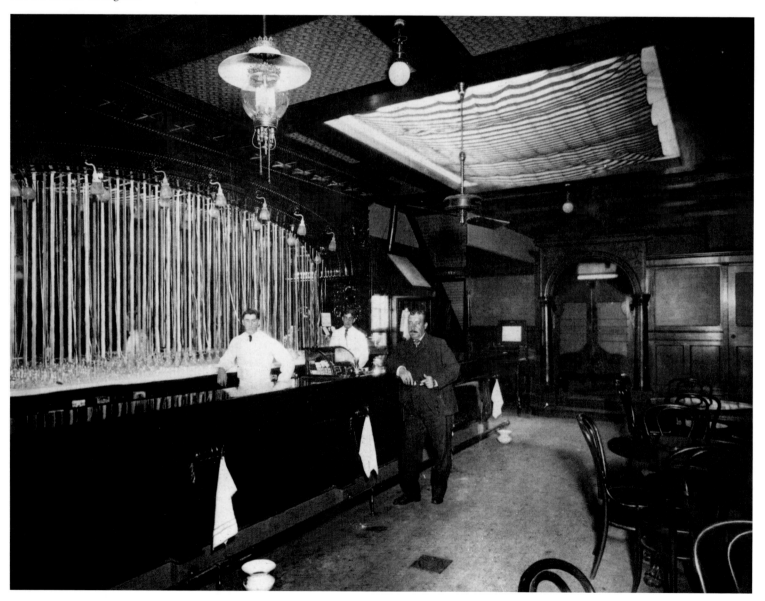

The steel railroad trestle installed in 1891 replaced the earlier wooden trestle, but it was too weak for heavier trains and collapsed in 1904.

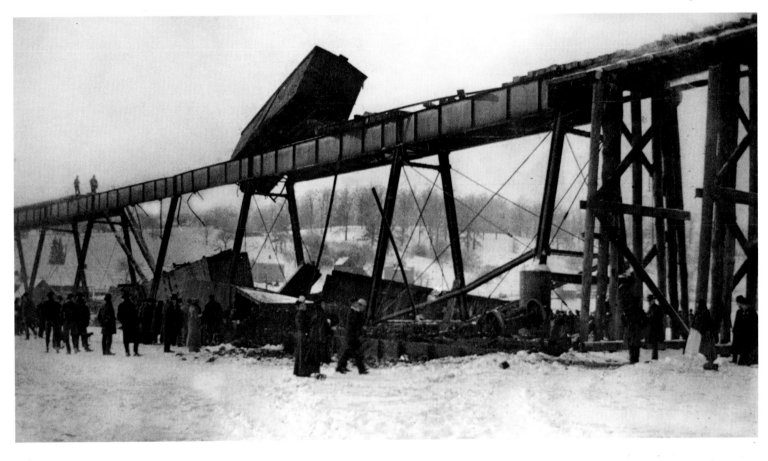

The Brotherhood of Painters and Decorators float is shown on North Ashley Street in 1901 during "the biggest parade Ann Arbor ever seen," as it was described on the back of the photograph. Exactly the purpose of that parade, or whether it was topped by subsequent parades, has long since been forgotten.

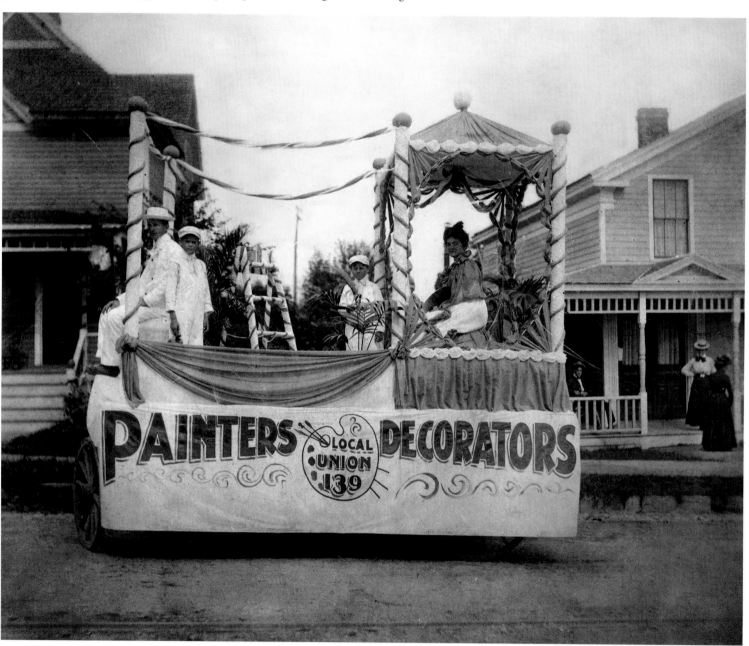

The Ann Arbor Central Mills, ca. 1900. This building, located on South First Street between Liberty and Washington, replaced the clapboard structure that previously housed the Central Mills. The northernmost building in this compound was built for use as mill offices, and now houses the Blind Pig, a popular nightclub and music venue.

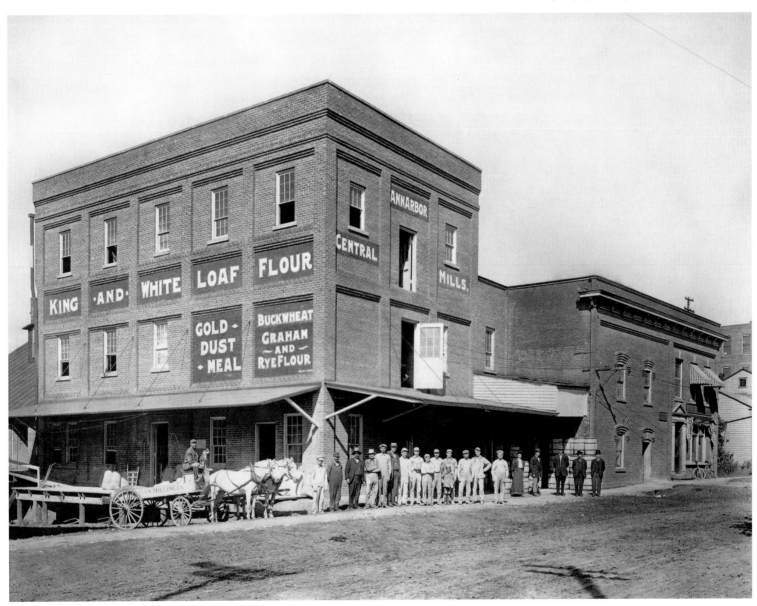

The Ann Arbor Golf Club, facing southwest from the first tee, ca. 1903. In 1899 the club leased, and then in 1903 purchased, this large tract of land at 400 East Stadium Street. It is one of the oldest continuously operating golf clubs in the country.

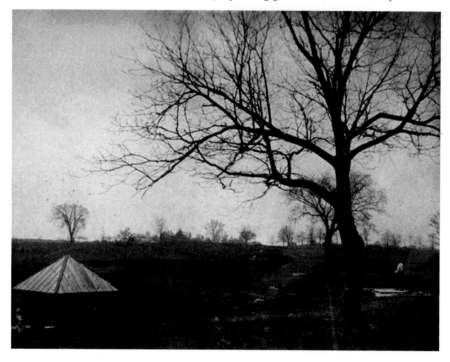

State Street, from the northwest corner of Central Campus, in 1907. The State Street area, despite all its changes, remains remarkably the same today as it was one hundred years ago. The only difference (besides the substitution of automobiles for horse-drawn carriages) is that today these buildings house different stores, including a coffee shop and several cafes.

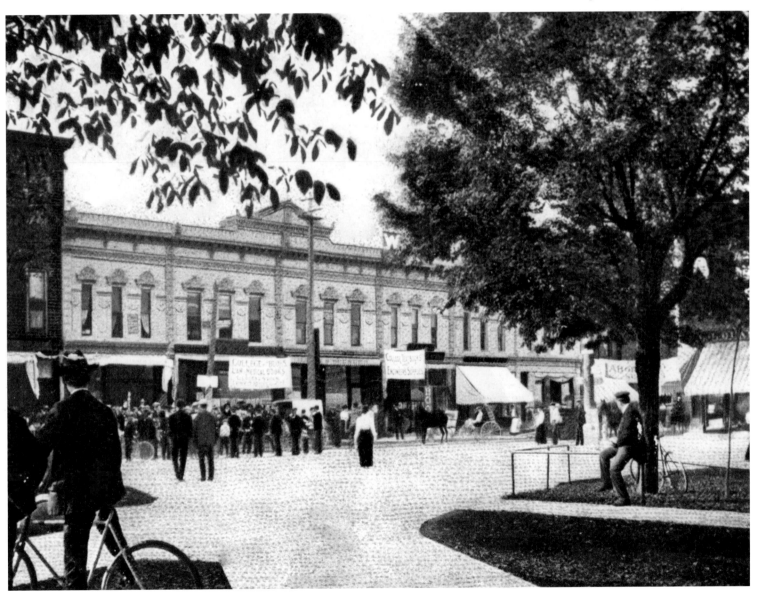

A band concert at Island Park, ca. 1900-1910.

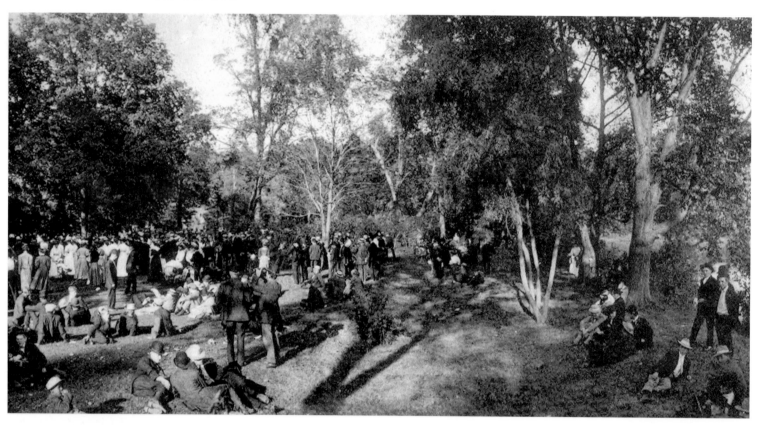

Main Street, facing southeast from Huron, in 1907. At left,
Goodyear's Drugstore offers physicians' supplies.

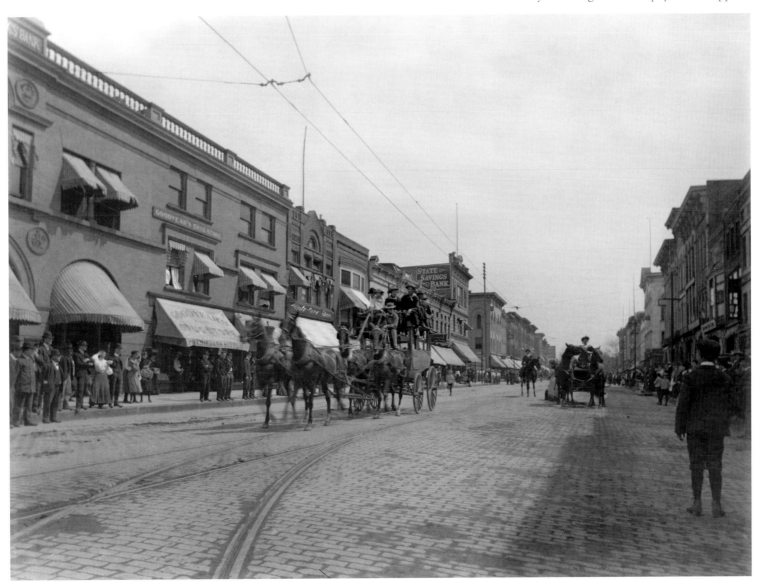

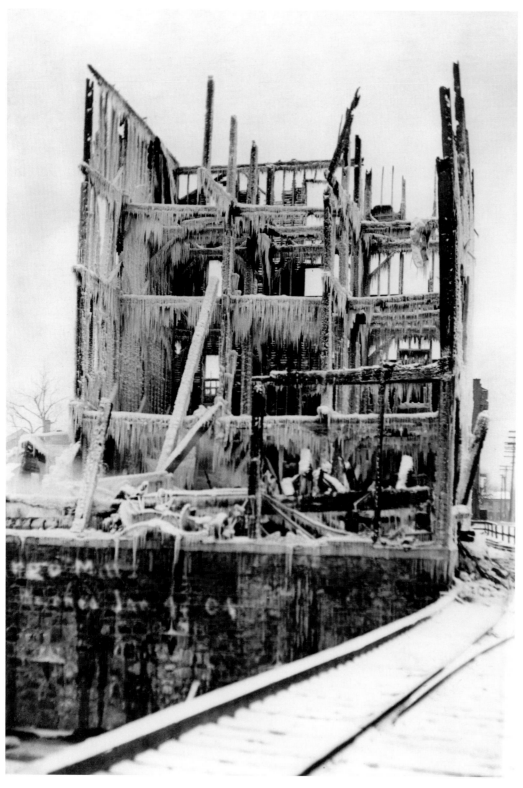

Aftermath of the Argo Mills Fire of 1904. The mills, located on the northern side of the Huron River at Broadway, burned down that January. The Michigan Milling Company, its owner, then built the Argo Powerhouse on this site to power its other mills. The facility was purchased by the Eastern Michigan Edison Company in 1905.

Hose Company No. 3 leaves the engine house for a fire in 1906. The firehouse was built in the Italian villa–style in 1882-83 and designed by Detroit architect William Scott. Today this building houses the Ann Arbor Hands-On Museum.

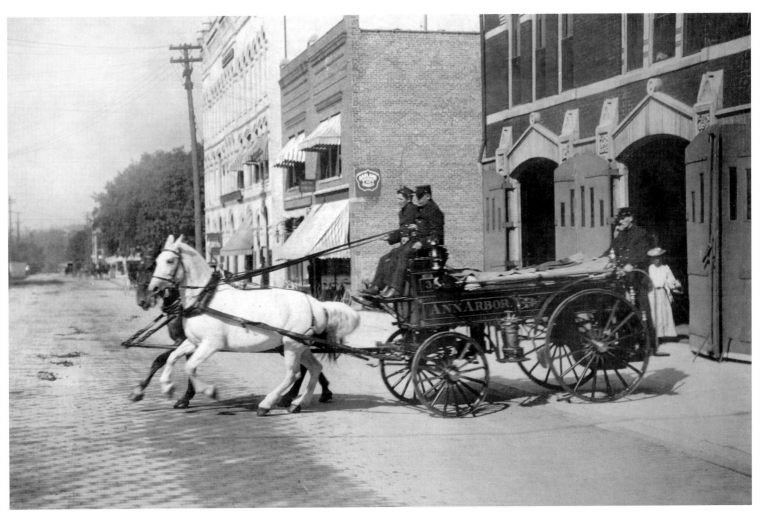

The West End Rifle Team practices their marksmanship in Schuetzenbund ("Shooting Team") Park, now Fritz Park, on Pauline Boulevard, ca. 1910.

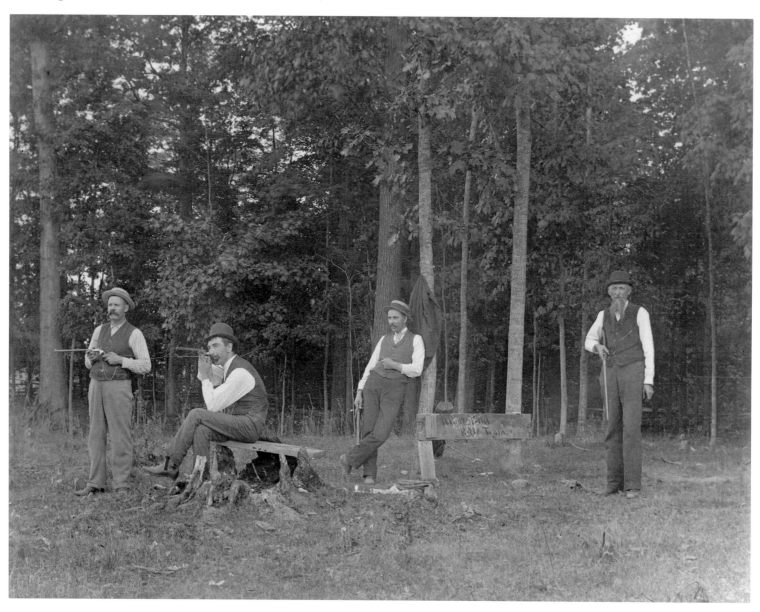

Main Street, facing south from Huron, in 1910. Every kind of transportation available to townspeople of the time is visible here, except automobiles, which hadn't yet grown popular. There are horse-drawn carriages, a streetcar, bicycles, and people on foot. By 1908, although more than 15,000 people called the city home, only forty automobiles plied city streets.

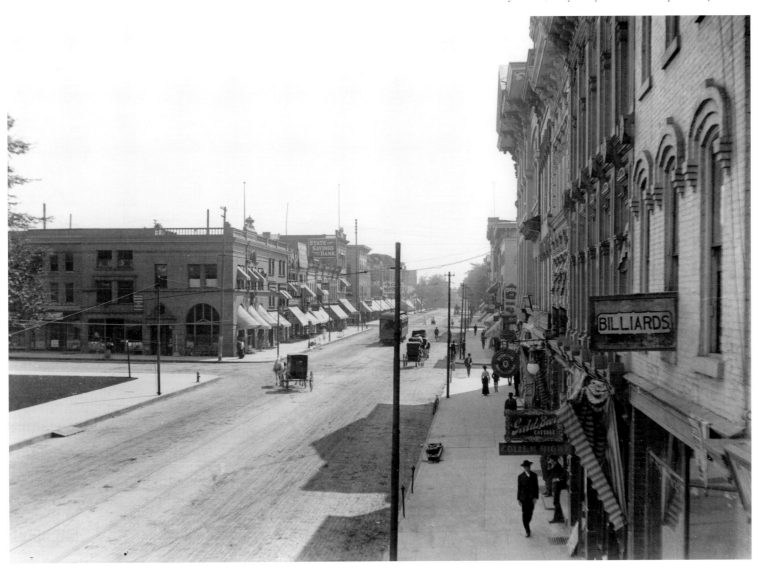

A man fishes near fallen trees on the Huron River, ca. 1905-10. Bass and bluegill are still reeled in daily by those who enjoy fishing the Huron.

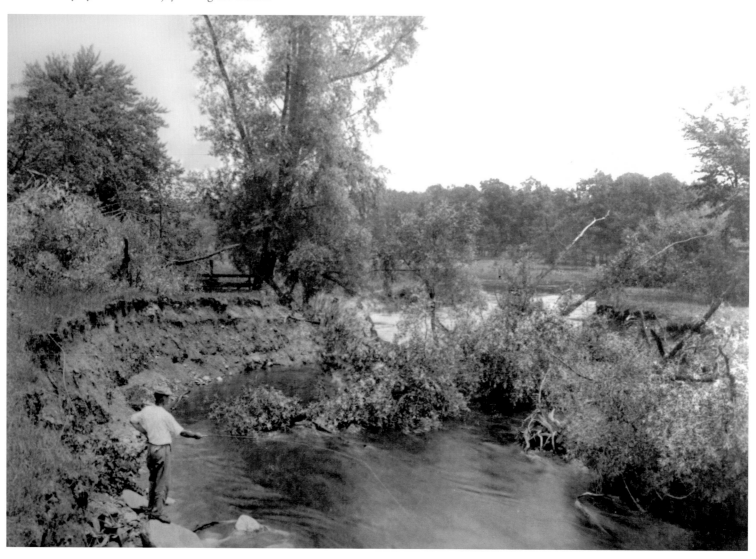

This image was used to advertise Michigan Union's county fair for 1908. The Michigan Union was an organization of male students founded in 1904 to coordinate and maintain a student union. They sponsored a variety of social events, including the popular Union Opera, and activities such as this county fair.

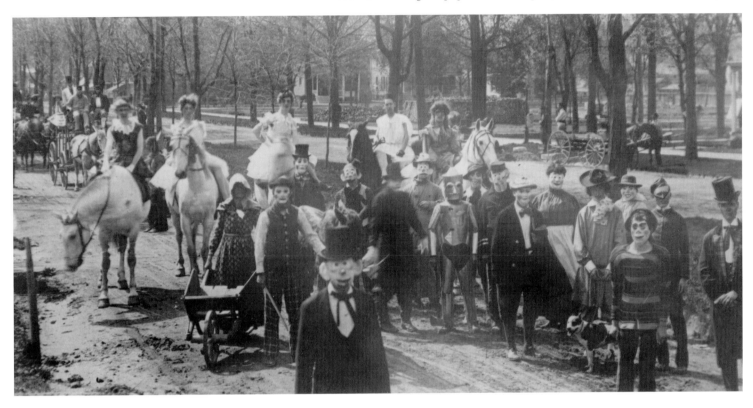

The Ann Arbor Fire Department poses for a photograph in 1908.

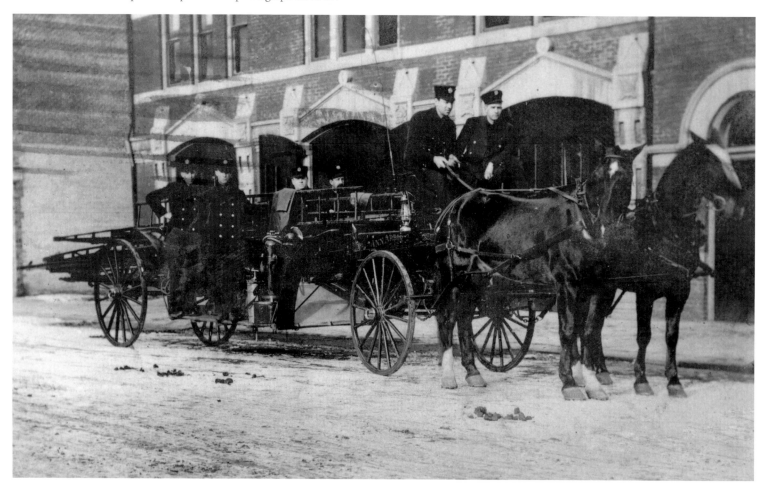

The Ann Arbor Police Department in 1908. Organized in 1871, the department fulfilled the wishes of the townspeople by attempting to control the rowdy behavior of students and warn of fires. Previously, the city's law enforcement duties had been assigned to a part-time marshal and ward constables.

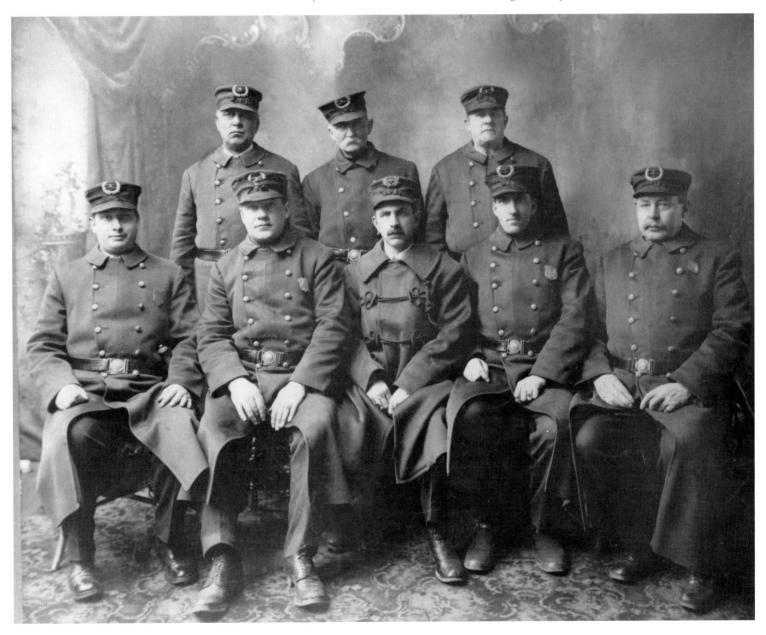

A boat livery, ca. 1901-16. Located on the Huron River at North Main Street, this private company rented boats to University of Michigan students and visitors. Boating and canoeing on the Huron River continues to be a popular recreational activity.

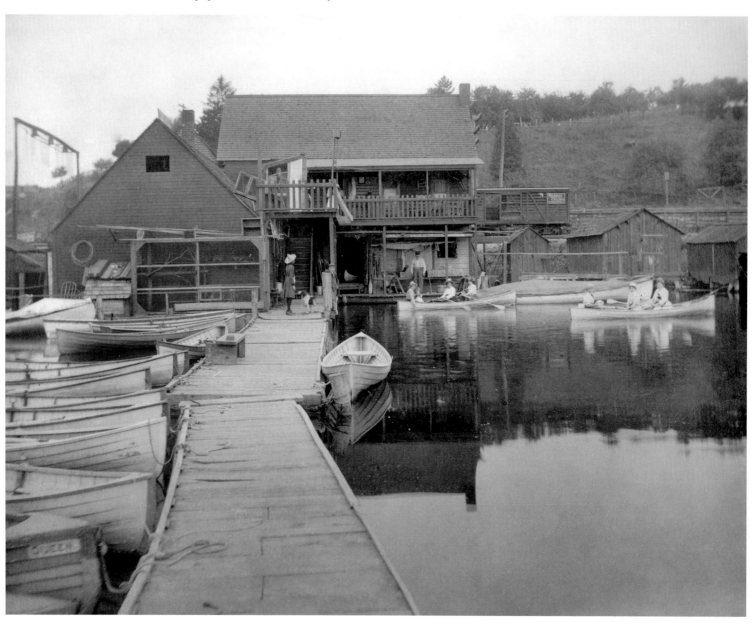

View of a train accident on the Ann Arbor Railroad in 1908. The wreck occurred just north of the depot at 416 South Ashley Street. The Ann Arbor Railroad operated between Toledo, Ohio, and Frankfort, Michigan, bringing supplies to town and ferrying townspeople on short-distance trips.

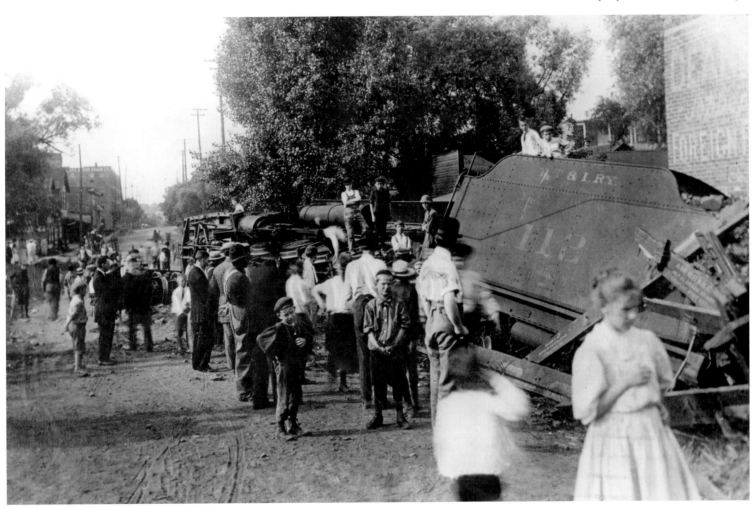

A Michigan Union circus parade in 1909. This procession, an example
of the social activities organized by the Michigan Union club, marched
south on State Street, attracting the attention of curious children. The First
Congregational Church, founded in 1876, can be seen behind the crowd on
the corner of State and William streets.

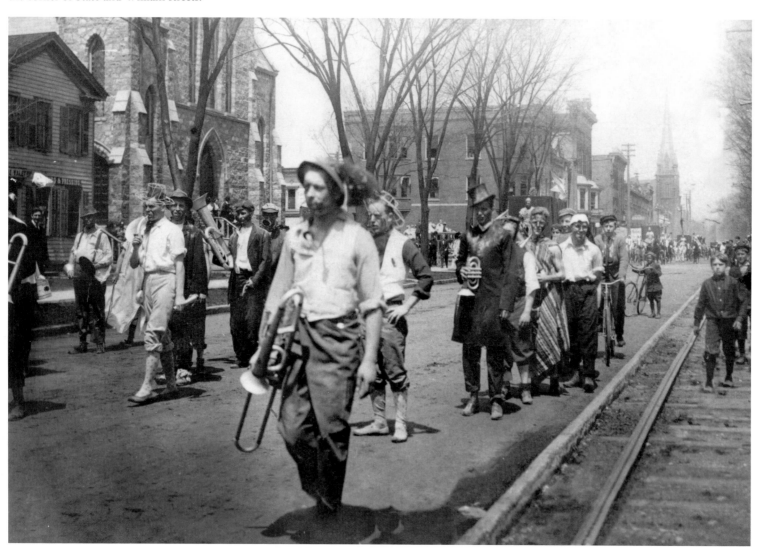

The Ann Arbor High School football squad practices at the fairgrounds in 1908. The area reserved for the county fairgrounds in 1908 is now the site of Burns Park.

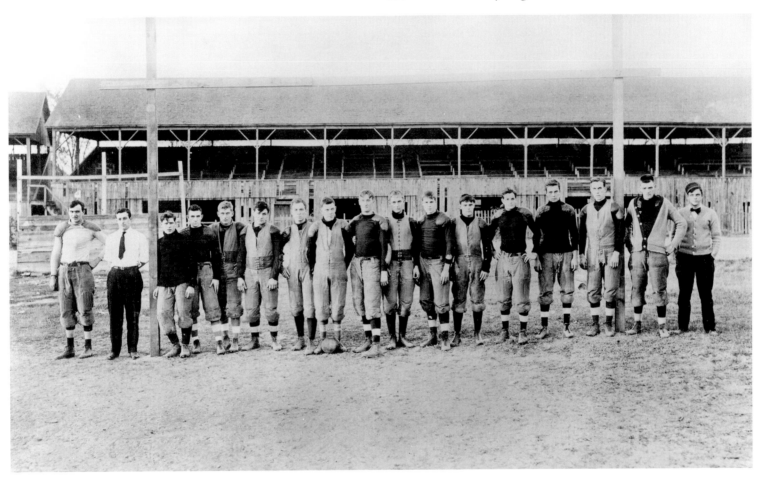

The Boulevard: Cedar Bend, above Island Park, ca. 1907.

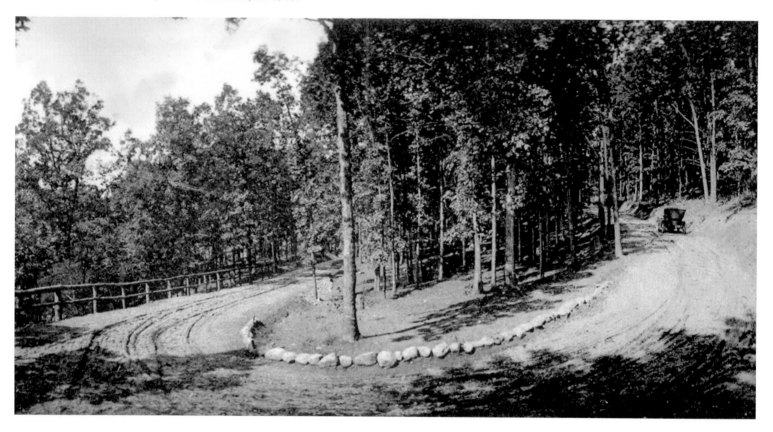

A delivery wagon at Fischer & Finnell's Cigar Company, South State Street at Packard, before 1910. This store served as an interurban stop, until the service ended in 1929. It still stands today and continues to be part of an important shopping district for students living south of campus.

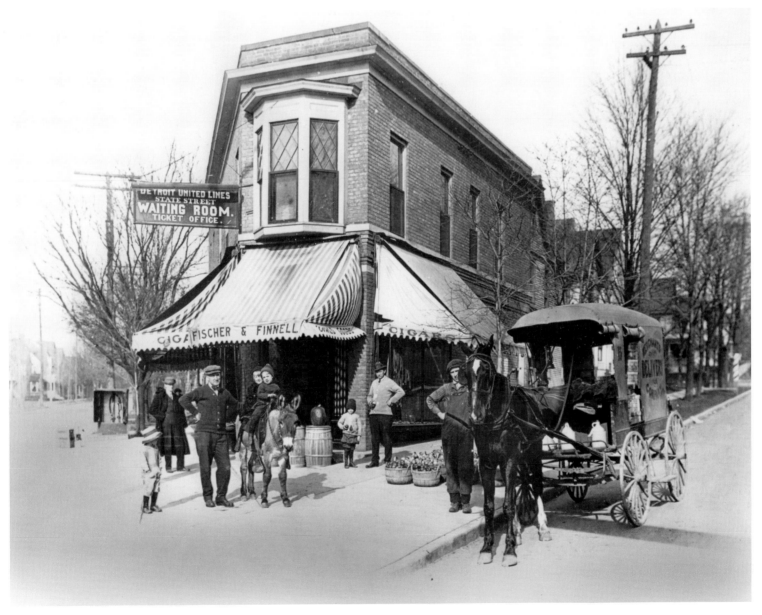

Huron Street, facing east from Main Street, in 1907. Opened in 1883, the Farmers and Mechanics Bank, on the corner, was partly demolished by a crash of the interurban in 1927. Bicycles had gained in popularity by this time, as evidenced by their presence on the street.

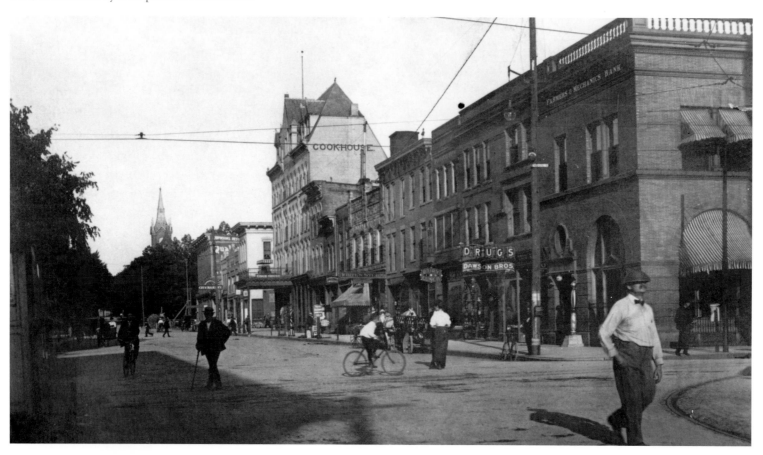

A Walker Livery cutter in 1910. Winter travel was easier by cutter than by buggy, especially in rural areas where snow removal was difficult.

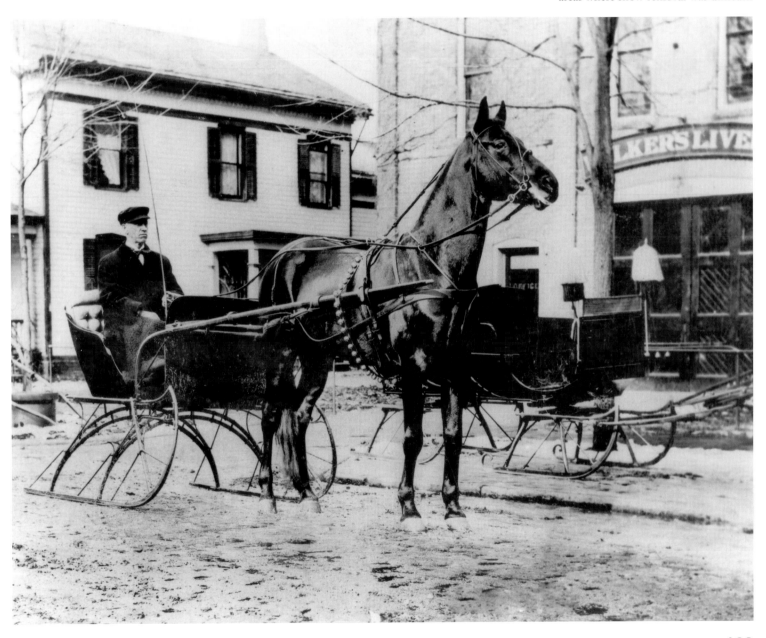

Hose Company No. 1, Ann Arbor Fire Department, 1906. In spite of a number of particularly devastating fires, including the Argo Mills fire of 1904, the townspeople of Ann Arbor repeatedly voted down proposals for the fire department to switch to motorized fire engines. Finally, in 1915 a fire truck was procured for the department and the old horse-drawn engines were gradually phased out.

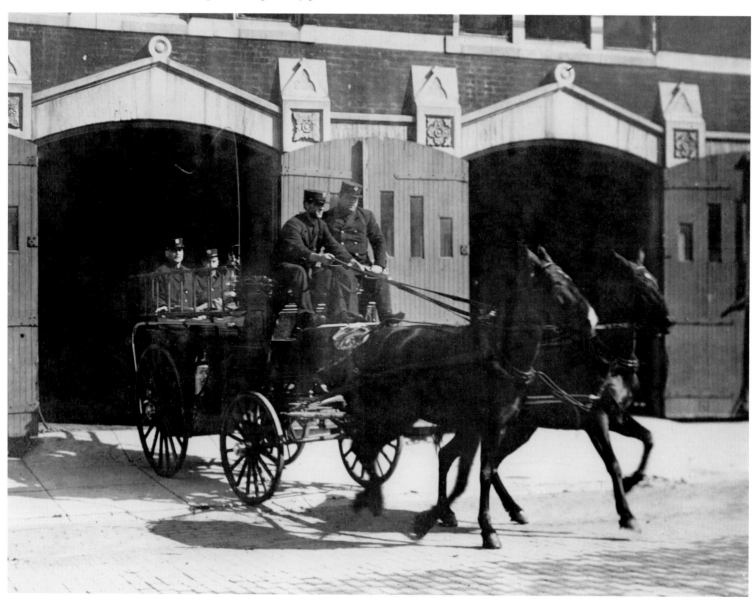

The Michigan Union advertises a minstrel show ca. 1910. In 1907 the student union had raised enough money to purchase the home of faculty member Thomas M. Cooley on State Street to use as its headquarters. In 1916, construction began on a new Michigan Union building, located on the same site.

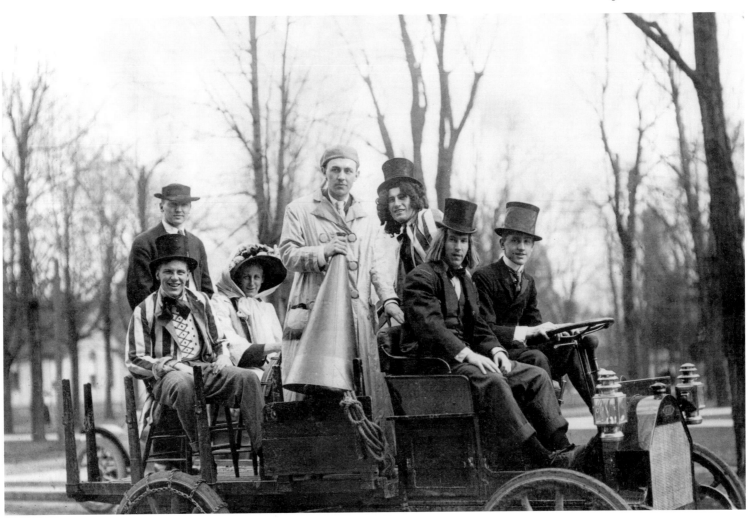

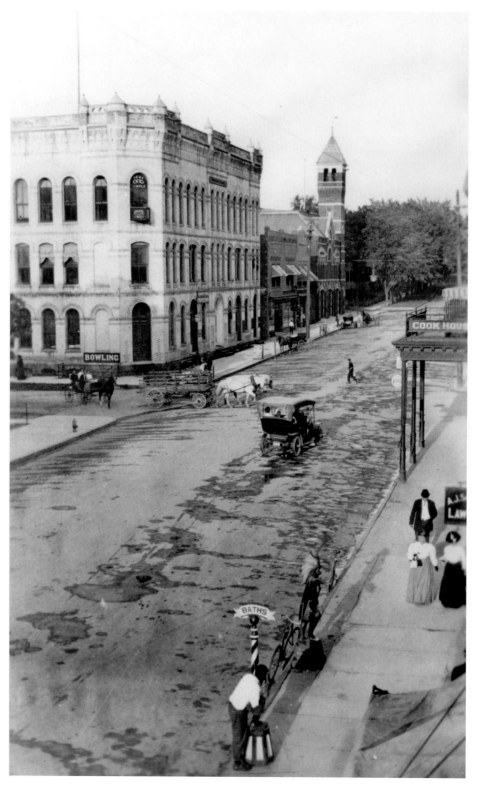

Huron Street and Fourth Avenue, facing east, ca. 1910s. The building across the street from the Cook House Hotel is the Hamilton Block (later known as the Cornwell building), built in 1882. It housed the Postal Telegraph Cable Co. on its first floor in the 1890s and a bowling alley at the time of the photograph. Visible down the street is the firehouse.

Construction of Barton Dam is under way in 1912. Barton Dam was the first of four dams constructed on the Huron River by Detroit Edison (along with its subsidiary, Eastern Michigan Edison Company) to supply the city with more hydroelectric power. The dam was designed by Professor Emil Lorch, head of the University of Michigan School of Architecture.

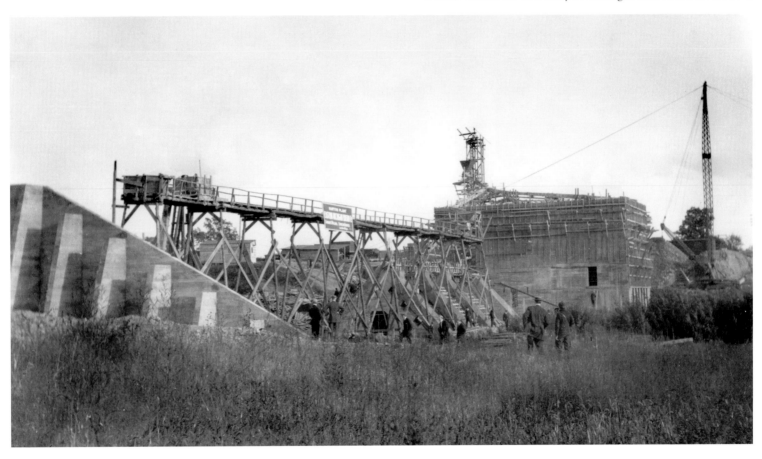

Otto's Band marches west on North University Avenue, east of State Street, in 1914. The Otto family was responsible for much of the music played at city gatherings and parades for the last part of the nineteenth century and the first part of the twentieth. Henry Otto was the conductor and leader of the band in the 1870s and 1880s, and his son Louis took over in the 1890s, continuing the tradition until after World War I.

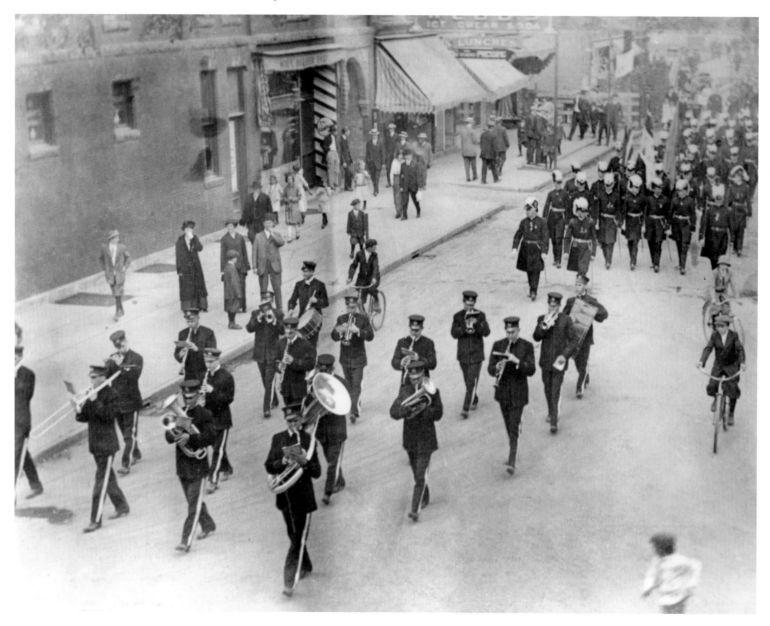

East Liberty Street ca. 1910. On the left streetcorner stands Allmendinger Music Shop. Allmendinger remained a big name in Ann Arbor commerce. By 1906 the manufacturer was producing 300 organs and 50 pianos a month.

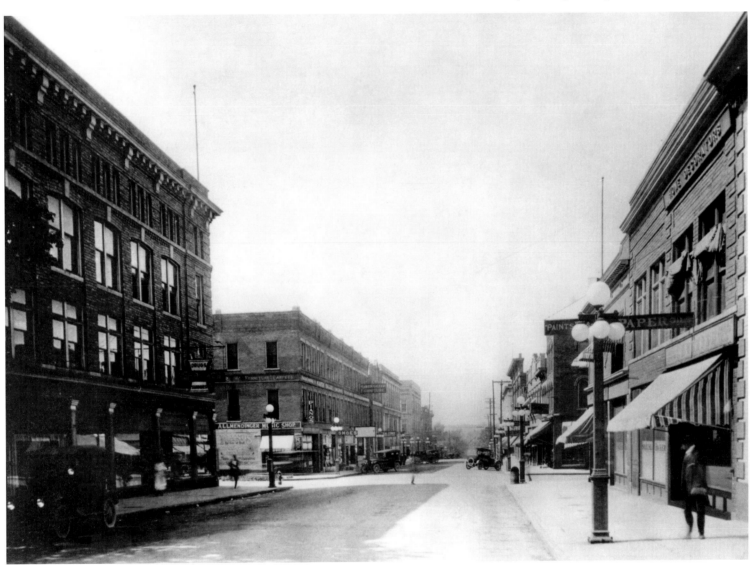

A Merchant's Delivery Company horse-drawn carriage in 1911. At this time horse-drawn vehicles were still prevalent, but most companies would switch to automobiles in the coming years.

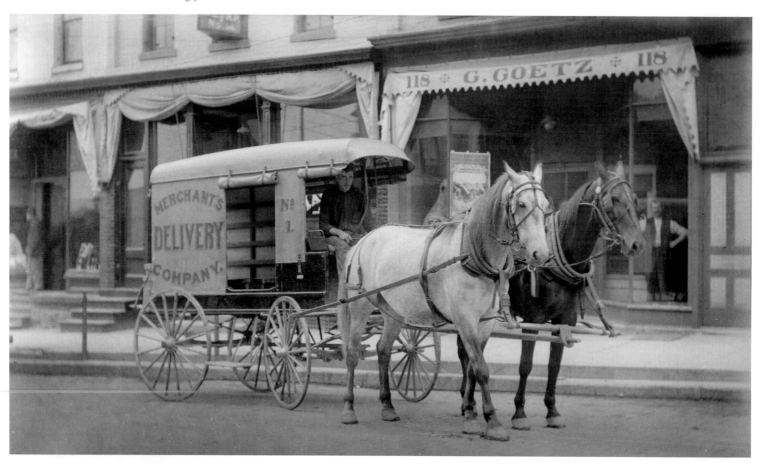

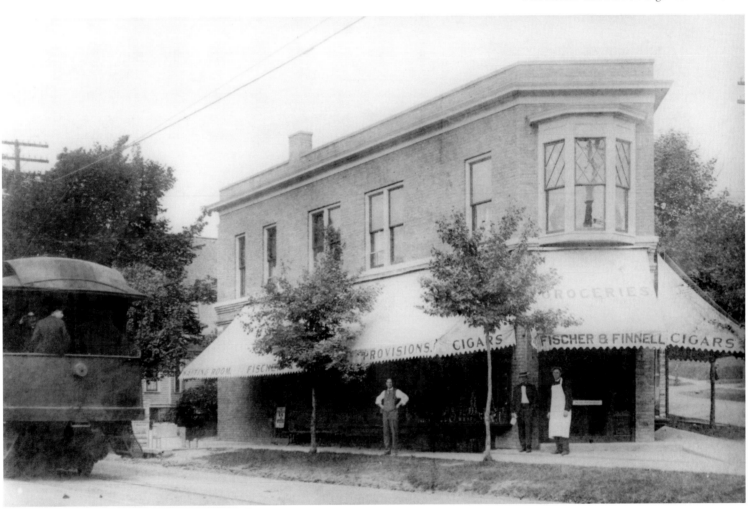

The Fischer and Finnell Cigar Store in 1910.

Walker's Livery was one of many businesses adapting to the ever more popular automobile. Abandoning the horse-drawn ways of the nineteenth century, the livery converted to car culture, becoming the Ann Arbor Taxicab and Transfer Company in 1914, shown here.

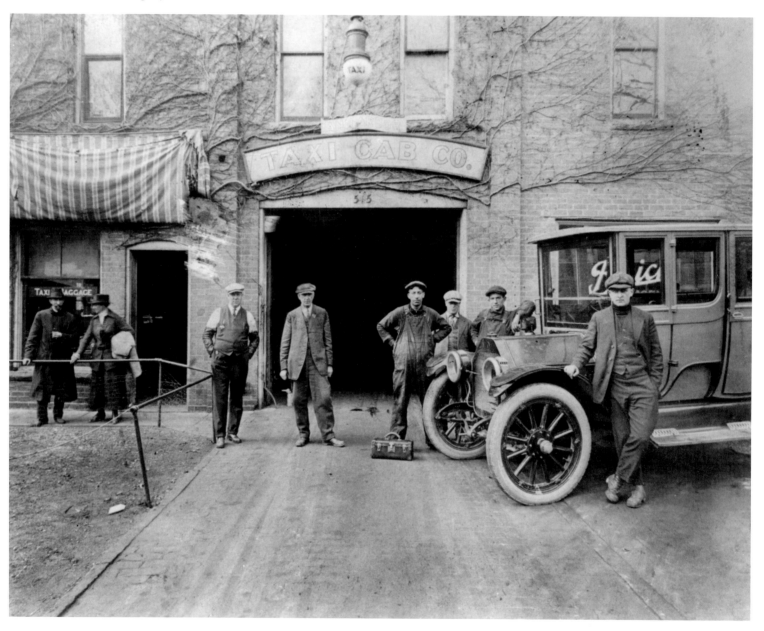

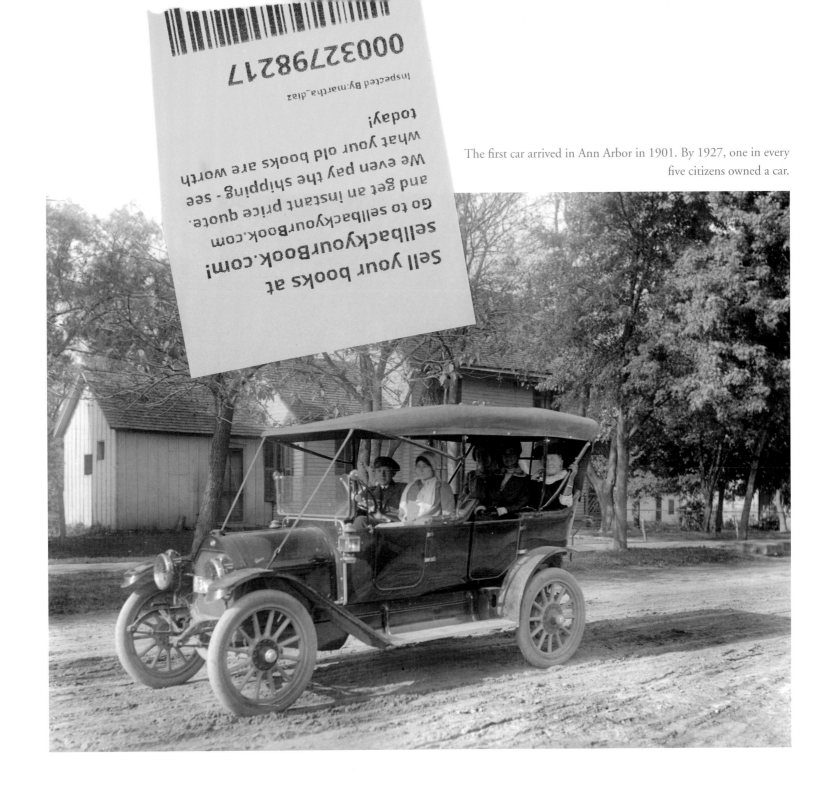

The first car arrived in Ann Arbor in 1901. By 1927, one in every five citizens owned a car.

Idlers pass the time beside the Huron River in 1910. Behind them, ads for Owl cigars and Staebler & Wuerth clothiers and furnishers decorate the building beyond the bridge.

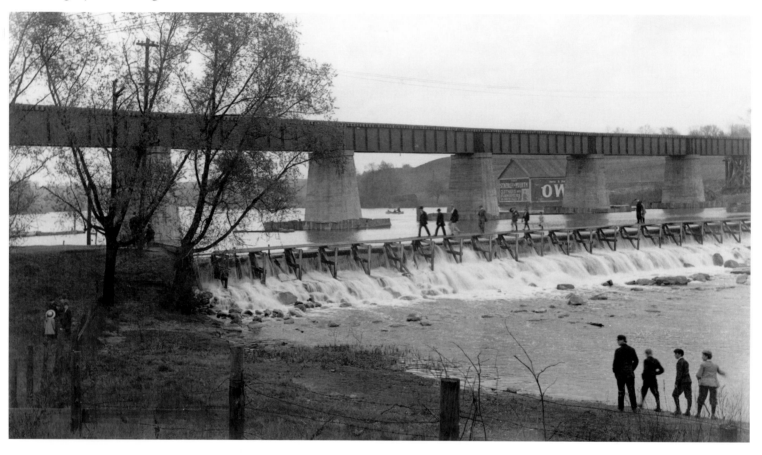

Motor Car #1 ran on gasoline, on a route from Ann Arbor to Whitmore Lake in the 1910s.

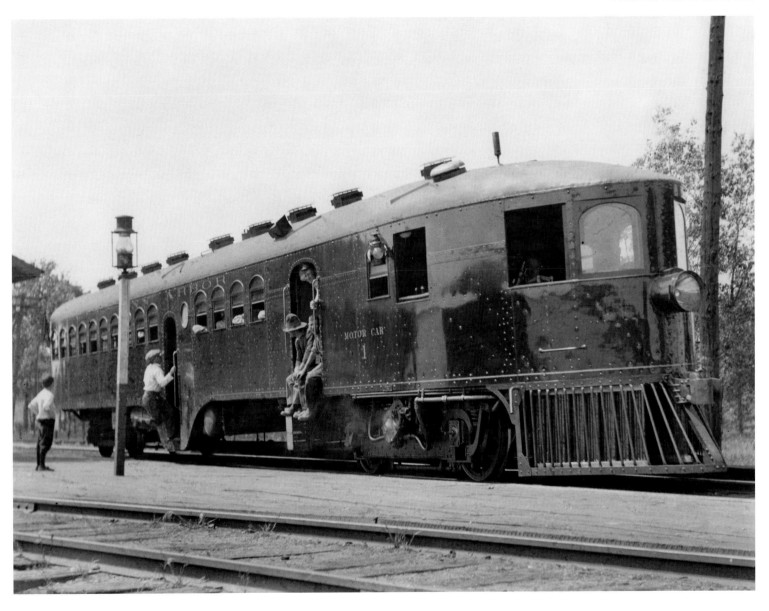

The Central Flyer, ca. 1910.

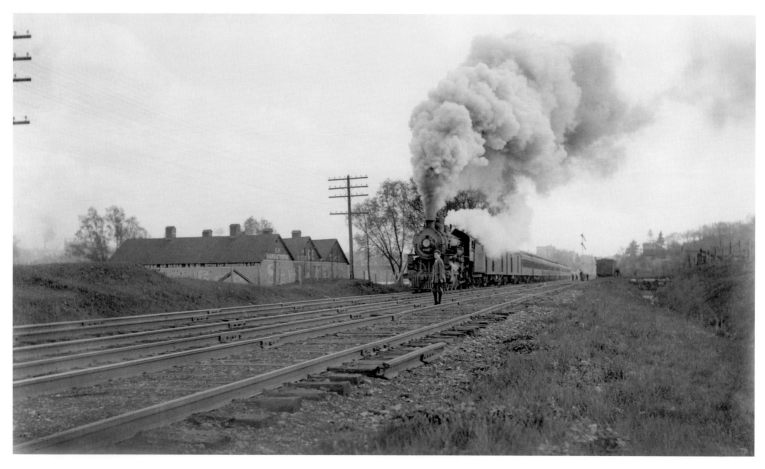

Circus animals are offloaded from the train at Michigan Central Station in 1913.

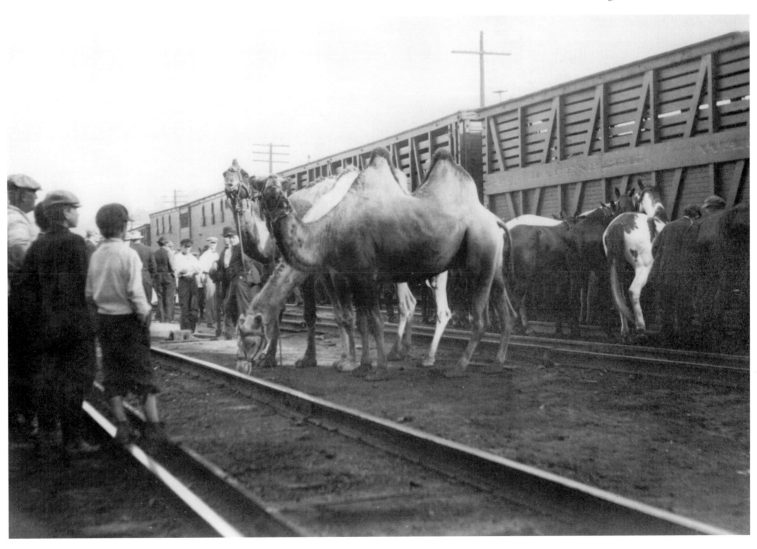

The Barnum and Bailey Circus was a popular attraction in many towns throughout the country. Until the 1930s, circus workers would camp out in Burns Park during their stay in Ann Arbor.

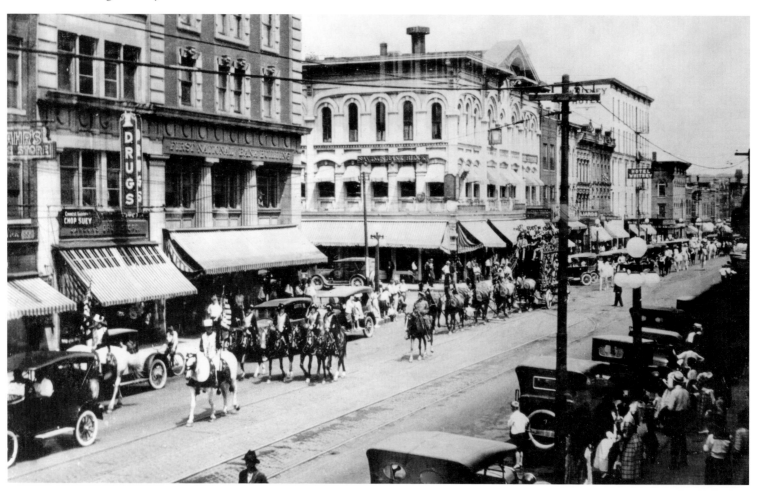

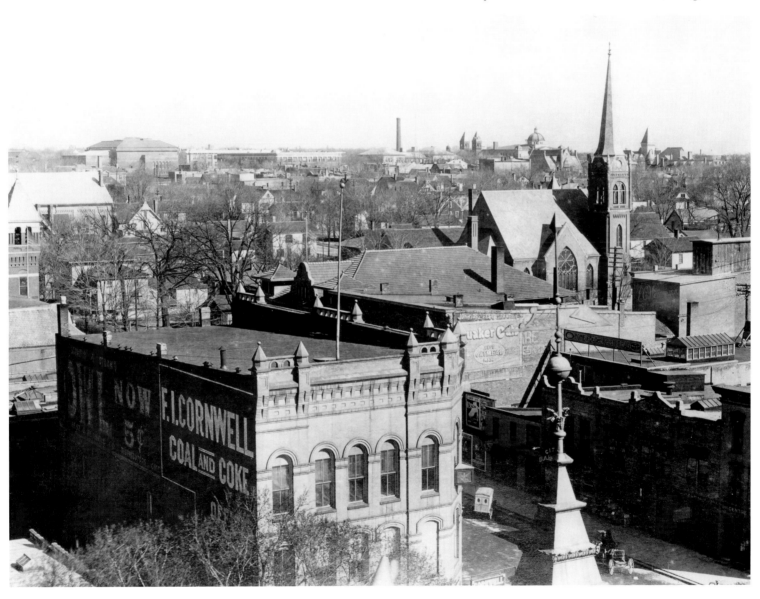

A rooftop view of town from the courthouse, facing southeast.

By the 1910s the University of Michigan had converted to the automobile.
The university relied mainly on utility vehicles, like this truck, for various
campus maintenance tasks.

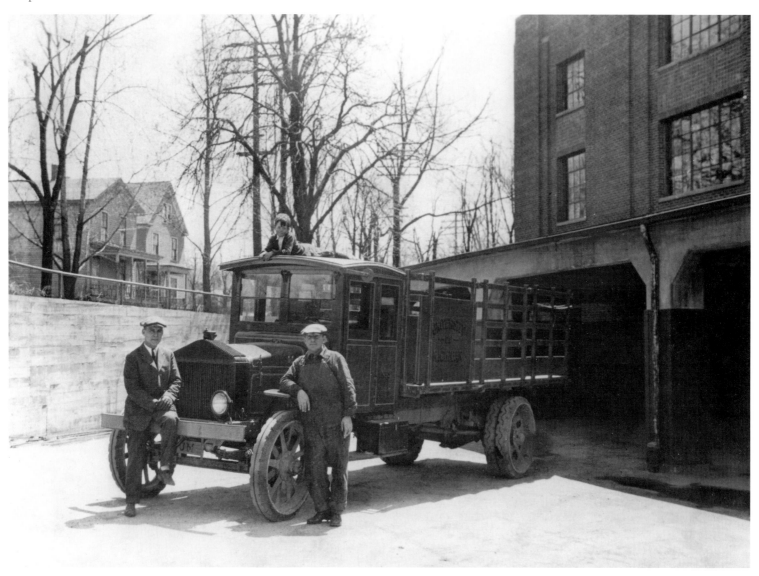

An early biplane prepares for take-off in 1910.

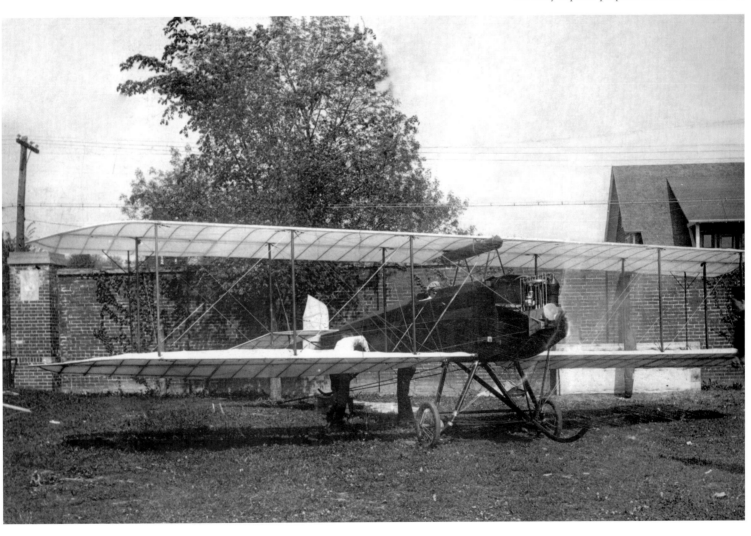

A rooftop view from the courthouse, facing north. The new *Ann Arbor Times-News* building stands in the foreground on Ann Street. The *Times News* was formed in 1908 out of a merger between the two local papers, the *Ann Arbor News* and the *Daily Times*. The *Times-News* was very well connected. By the early 1920s, the paper had, unusually, both a Morse and an automatic telegraph wire running into the offices.

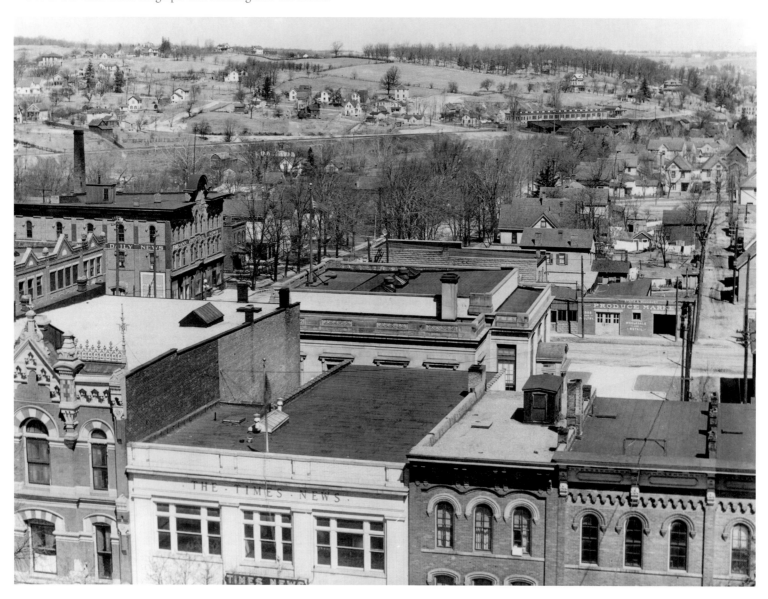

A 1925 history of Ann Arbor praised the city's schools: "Because Ann Arbor is the seat of one of the country's largest universities, something out of the ordinary might reasonably be expected of the public school system of that city. One has to live but a short time in Ann Arbor to know that this expectation has been realized." Miss Lily E. Goodhew and her class pose for a photograph at the Donovan School in 1911.

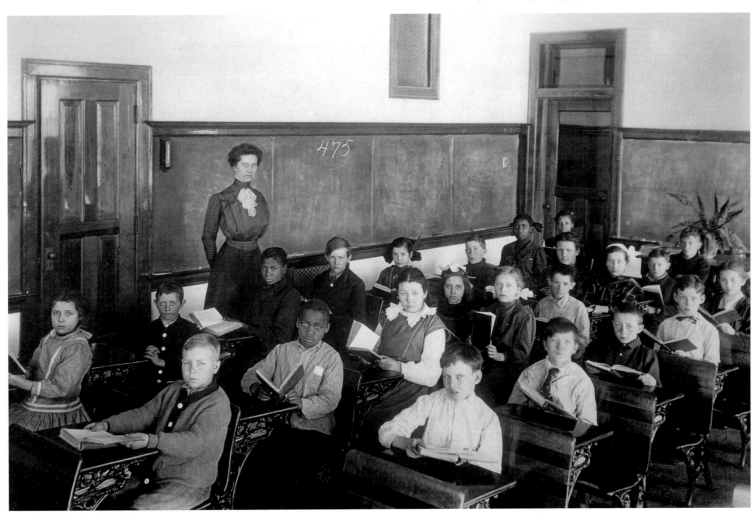

Long a symbol of local civic pride, the 1882 fire station continues to stand at Huron
Street and N. 5th Avenue in its original form with no significant structural alterations.
It was listed on the National Register of Historic Places in 1972.

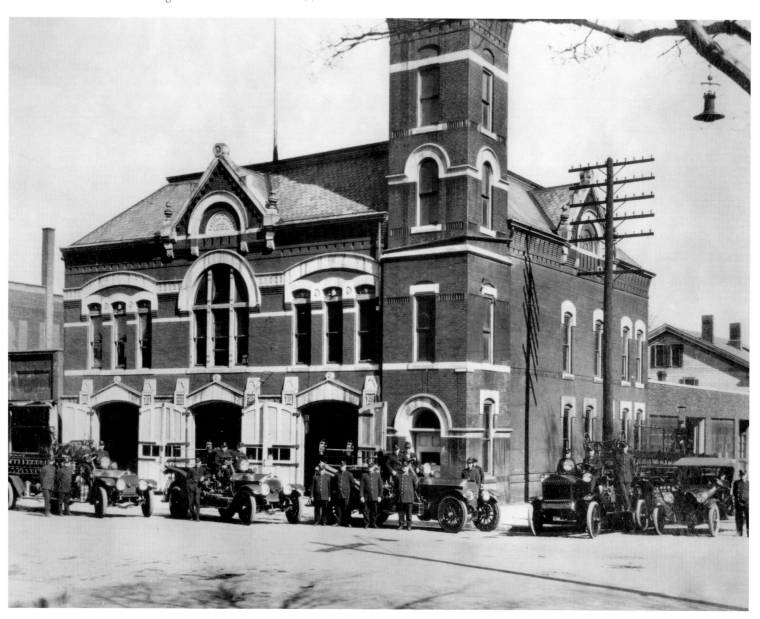

A Cousins & Hall Florists delivery truck. The company had its own greenhouses on the corner of South University and Haven Street, now the location of the School of Education.

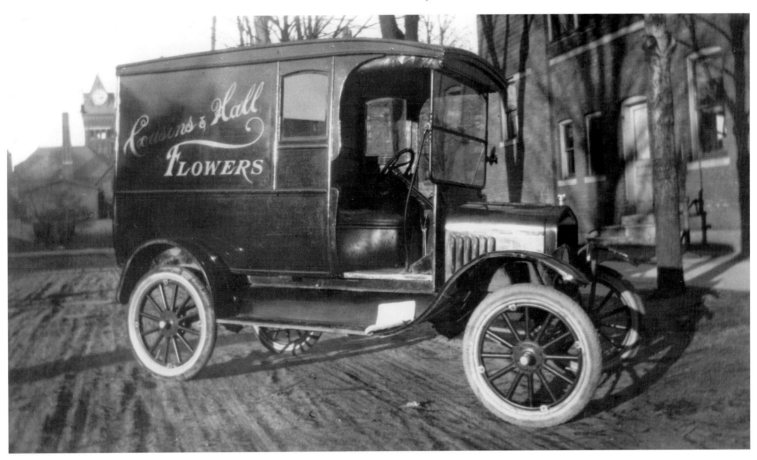

The Huron River is the largest waterway in Ann Arbor and flows to the southeast through town toward Ypsilanti from its origin in Oakland County.

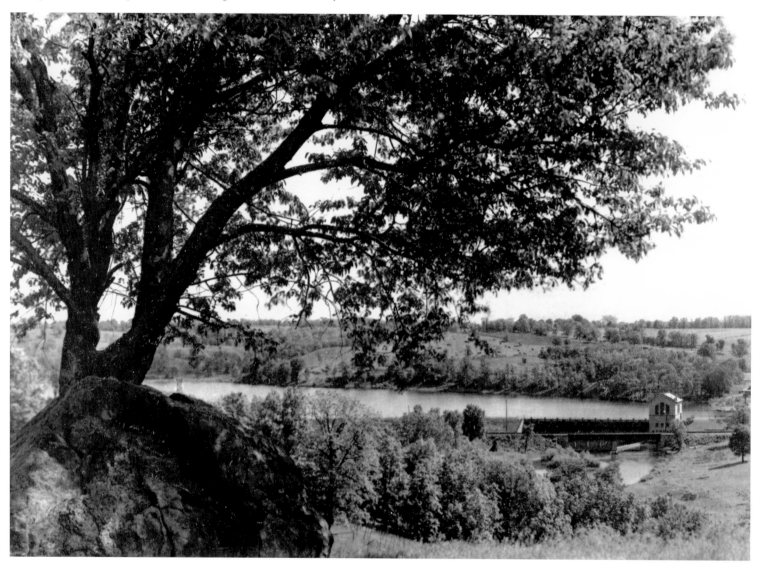

The Merchant's Credit Association holds a banquet at the Allenel Hotel.
The association would join with the Civic Improvement Association to form
an Ann Arbor Chamber of Commerce in 1918.

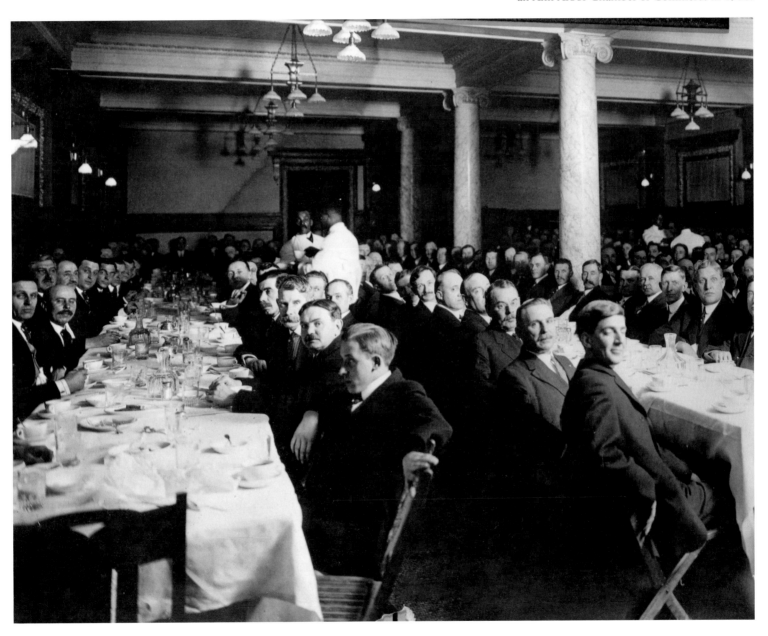

The corner of State Street and North University in 1914.

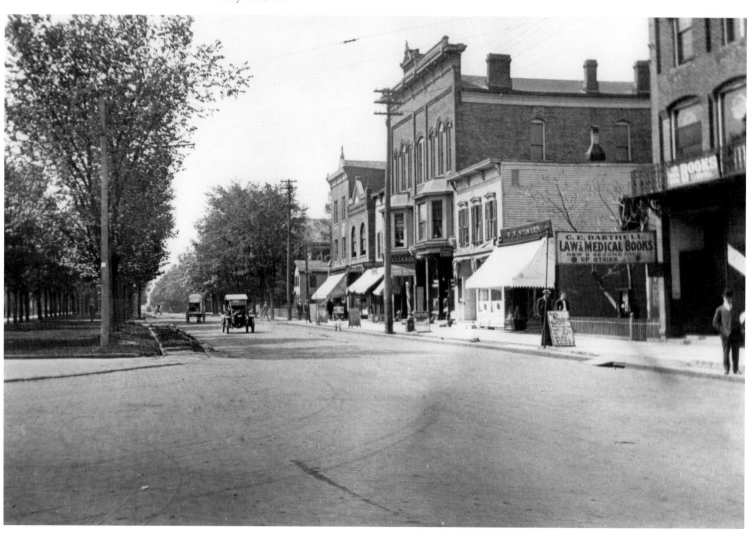

The influx of cars led to concerns about their maintenance and regulation within the city. In 1910 the city government adopted the first set of traffic laws, with special provisions not covered by previous state decrees.

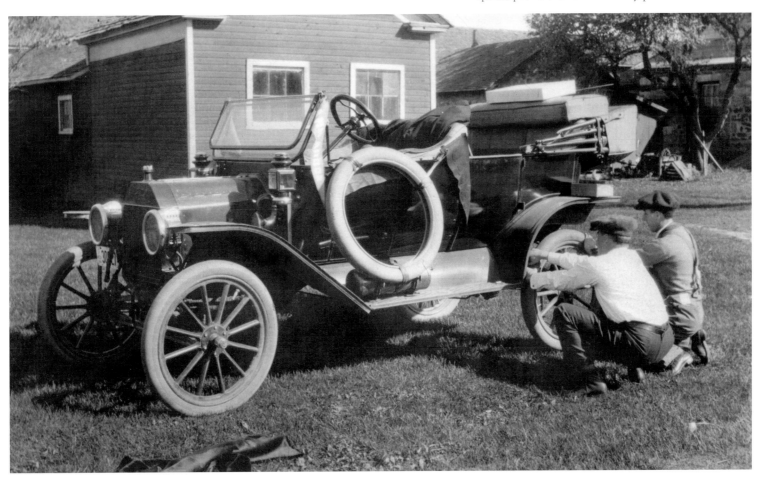

The local Young Women's Christian Association (Y.W.C.A.), ca. 1914. The YWCA was a powerful promoter of social and civic reform. In 1911, after hearing a report on the degraded moral state of the city, the YWCA formed the Social Purity Club, which organized curfews, limits on tobacco sales, neighborhood centers, and health education in schools.

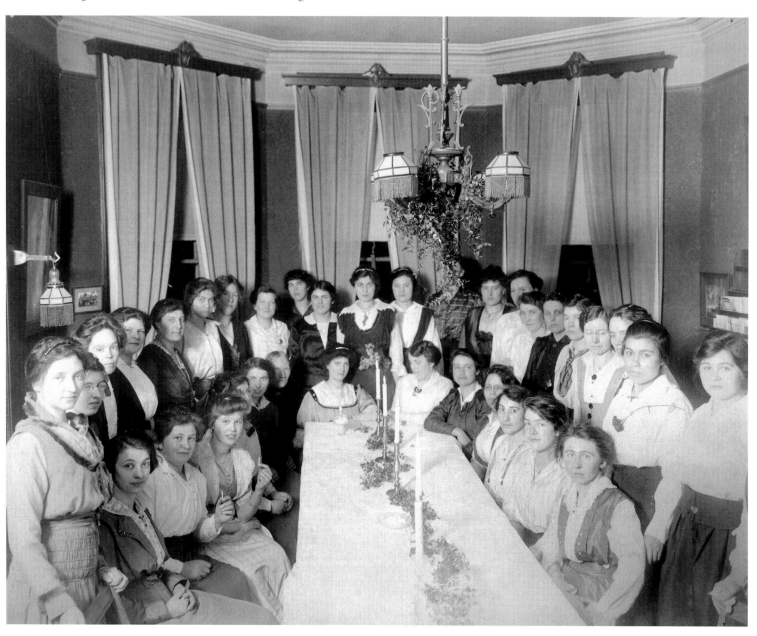

The Allenel, billed as a "European-Style" hotel, opened in 1911 under the ownership of the Nowlin family of Detroit.

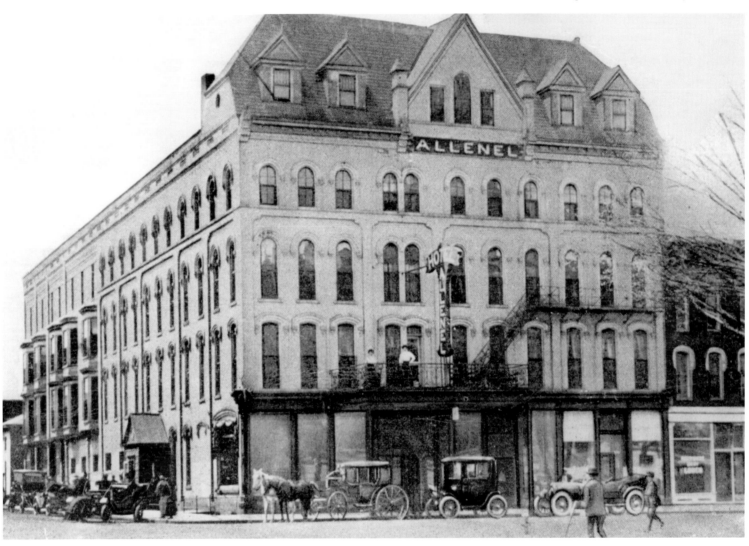

Three men in a boat on the Huron River.

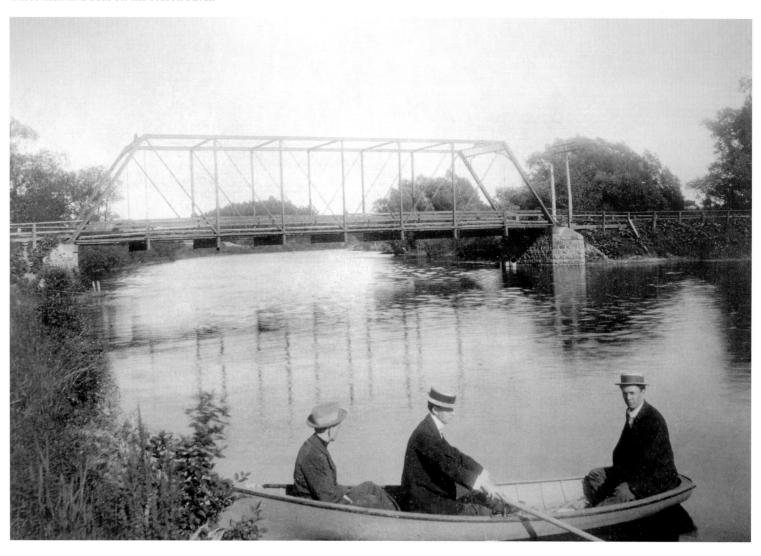

The staff of B. St. James Dry Goods and Notions, at 126 South Main Street, in 1909. The woman standing third from right is Bertha Muehlig, then the store's bookkeeper. Two years later, Muehlig would buy the store, renaming it Muehlig's. A 1924 history of the city said that "she is a native of Ann Arbor, and one of which the city can be proud."

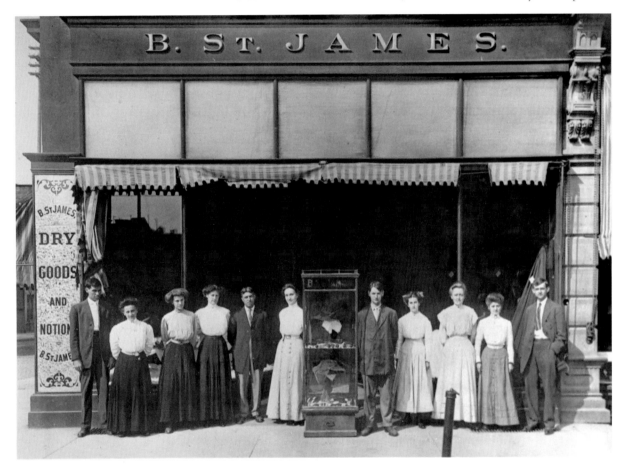

Don Gregory, a local airplane-enthusiast, flew his plane onto the roof of a ladder factory near Ferry Field in 1913. Miraculously, Gregory survived the accident without injury.

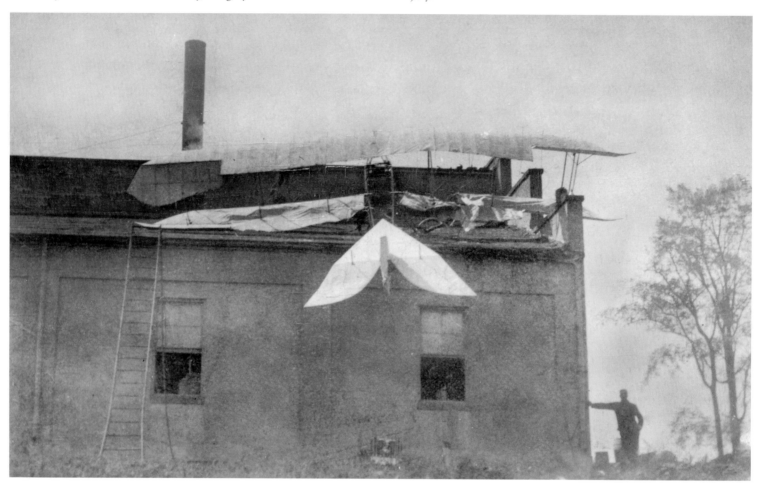

Van's Marine Band is on parade in 1916. Bringing up the rear are the Boy Scouts of America. Behind those assembled are an abstract office, the Y.M.C.A., and the Square Deal Garage.

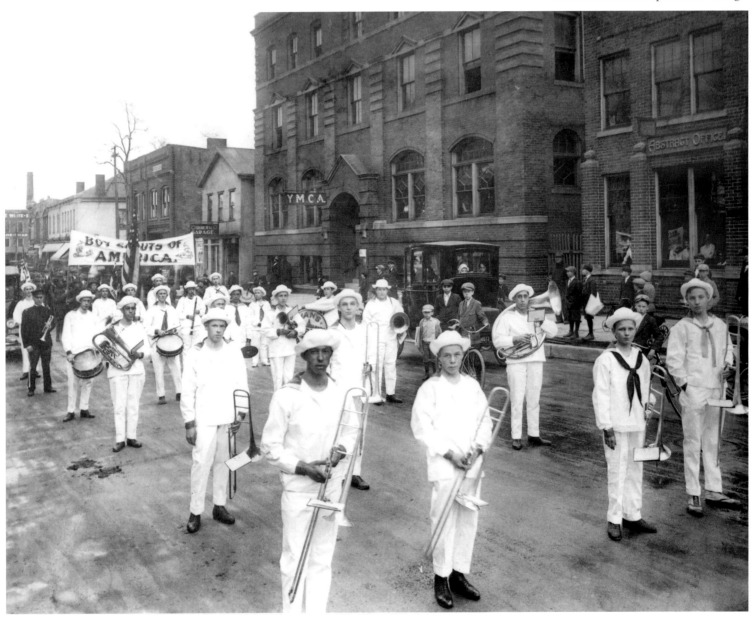

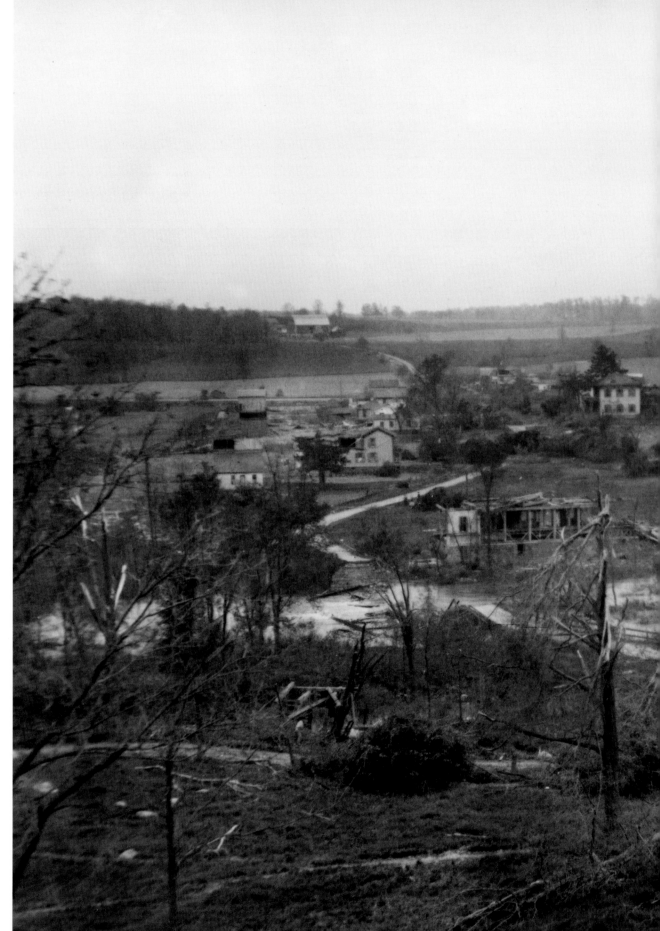

In 1916, a tornado ripped through Delhi, northwest of Ann Arbor along the Huron River.

136

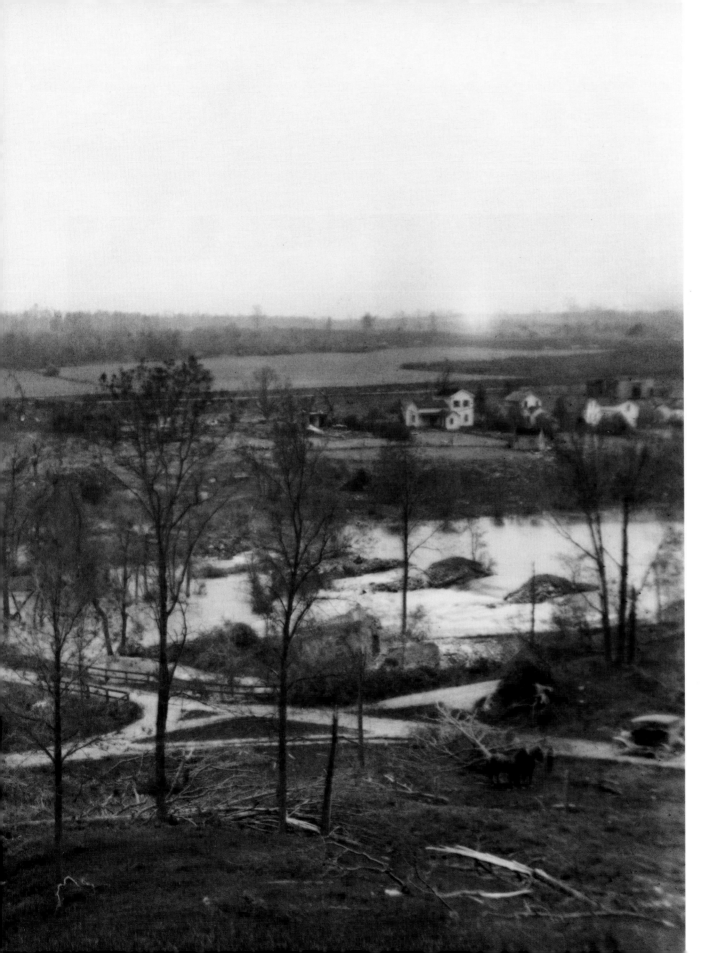

137

Camp Birket, in 1917. Thomas Birket, a resident of Dexter, operated a summer camp for boys on the shore of Big Silver Lake, starting in 1912. In 1920 he deeded his fifteen acres to the Y.M.C.A., which continued to run the camp.

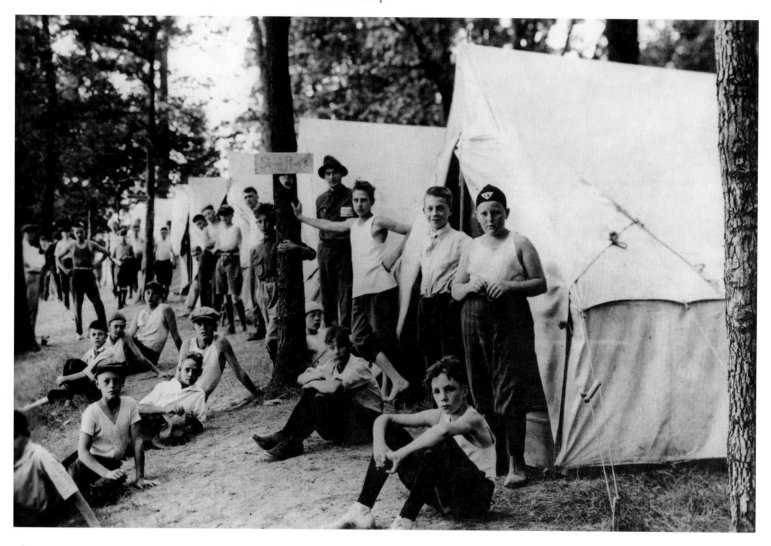

Staebler advertises Reo automobiles. The Staeblers operated the first automobile showroom in Ann Arbor.

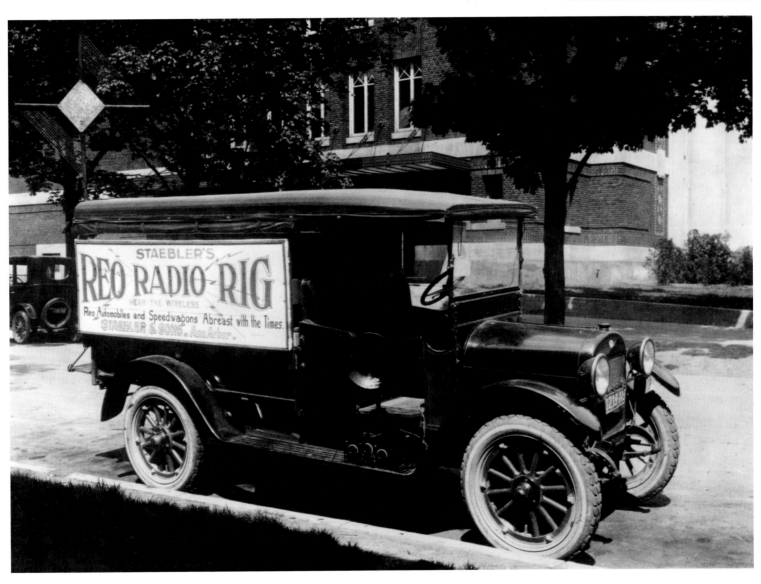

Hertler Bros. employees pose in front of the store on Labor Day. Hertler, located on South Ashley Street, was a purveyor of agricultural items such as hay, grain, feed, wood, salt, and farm tools.

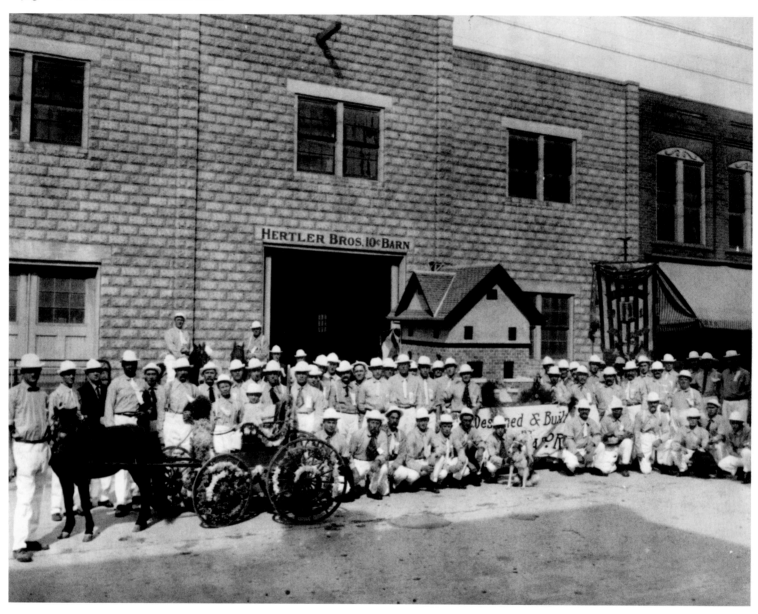

The Washtenaw County Chapter of the Red Cross played an integral role in organizing aid for World War I. In May 1918, the same month this parade took place, the local Red Cross gathered a total of 11,064 garments to be sent to France.

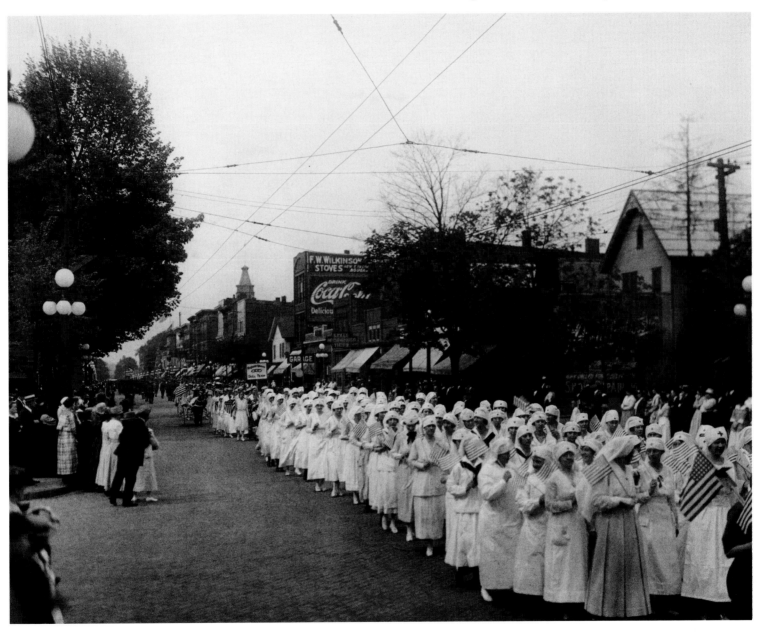

Armistice Day, marking the end of World War I, was vigorously celebrated in Ann Arbor. The day's festivities started with a bonfire on Main Street and Huron Street at 4 A.M., followed by a grand parade, pictured here. The parade included local bands, soldiers, the Salvation Army, boy scouts, local leaders, and schoolchildren. The procession culminated at Hill Auditorium, on North University Avenue.

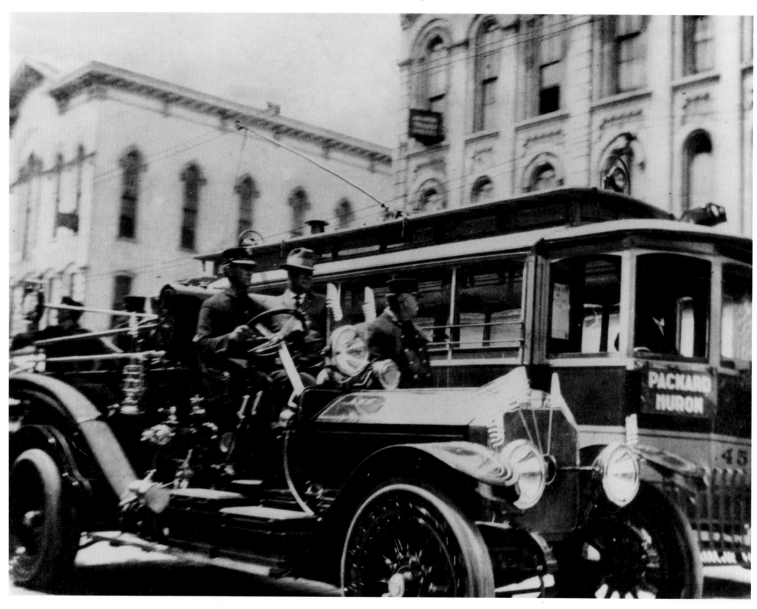

Musicians from the Ehnis Marching Band, ca. 1919. The band was a predecessor of the University of Michigan Band, and frequently played at UM football games.

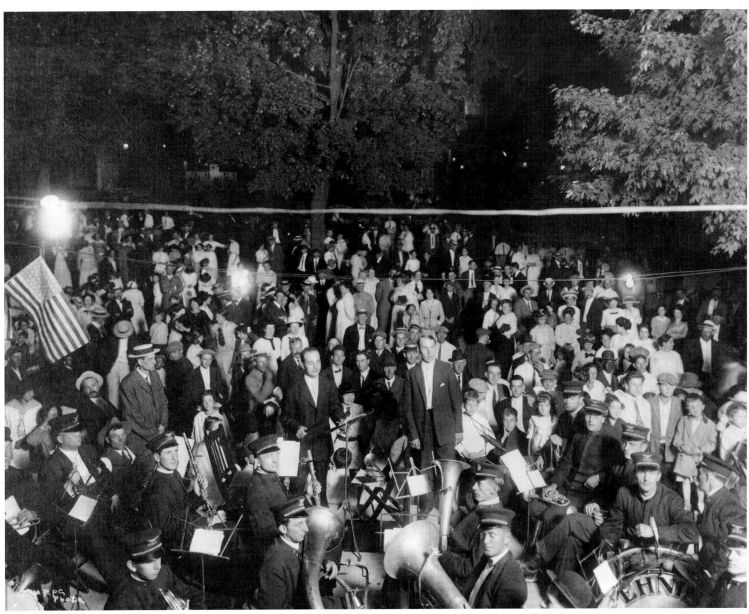

The Cadillac Garage Co., at 327-29 S. Main Street, in 1915.

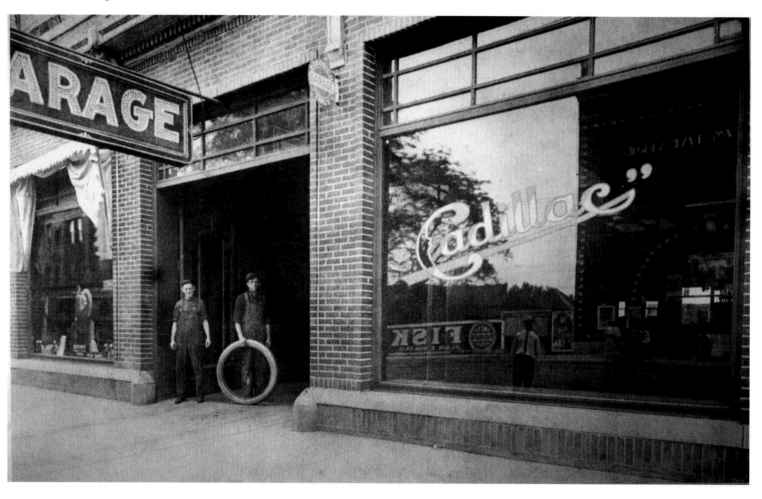

LOOKING INWARD

(1920–1939)

News of the end of World War I reached Ann Arbor on November 11, 1918, in the middle of the night. By the early morning hours, the town was awash in celebration of the end of the cataclysm, which had required the struggles and lives of many Michigan-born soldiers. The armistice was celebrated with a bonfire, songs, and a grand parade. The end of the war also ushered in a period of transition for the town, from manufacturing and immigration to one of civic growth and development.

Although local manufacturers had risen to the industrial challenges of war, they began to disband or relocate in the 1920s. Ann Arbor was becoming a residential town dominated by the presence of the University of Michigan, rather than an industrial powerhouse like its neighboring metropolis, Detroit. In 1922, concerned with creating a vision for its growth, the city obtained a report from the Olmsted Brothers architecture firm, famed for their design of New York City's Central Park. The report allocated different areas of the city for different purposes. The Westside was to be reserved primarily for workers' residences, while the neighborhood southeast of the university was intended for country homes. In 1923 the city passed its first zoning laws, placing restrictions on the commercial use of land. By the mid 1930s, the Ann Arbor Garden Club had launched a city beautification project. Workers migrated to Ann Arbor in this period, drawn not by industry, but by construction projects undertaken by the publicly funded city and university.

Perhaps owing to its increasingly retail-based economy and the presence of the university, Ann Arbor remained somewhat sheltered from the worst effects of the Great Depression. Unemployment nevertheless surged and many residents turned to civic relief programs. Municipal projects were undertaken to provide employment and wages for struggling locals. Many of today's parks in the city and along the Huron River were created by laborers for the Public Works Administration and the Works Projects Administration. By the mid 1930s, Ann Arbor had begun to recover, and continued to grow in size and significance as the 1940s approached.

The Machine Specialty Company Plant, located along the Huron River on North Main Street, is shown here in 1927. The company manufactured the unlikely combination of piston rings and radio equipment, on N. Main and on Wildt Street, employing about 50 men by 1925.

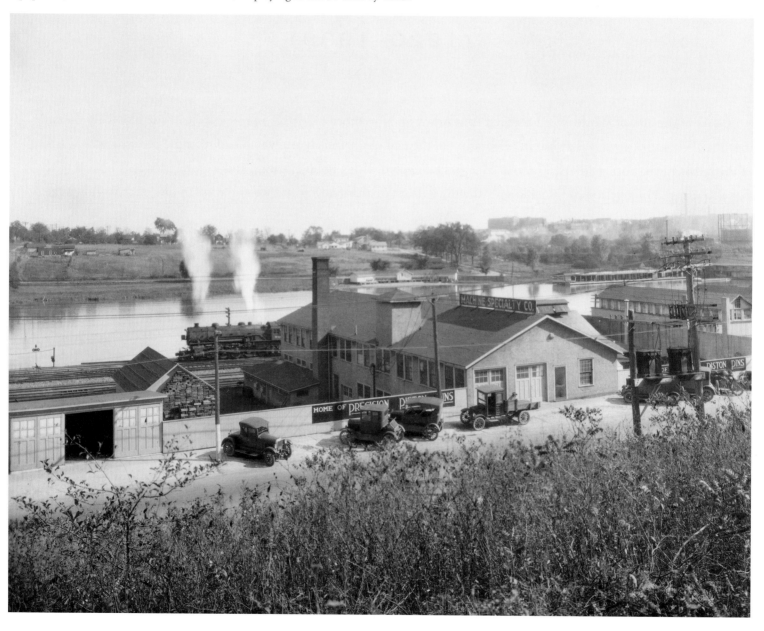

East Ann Street from 14th Street, ca. 1920.

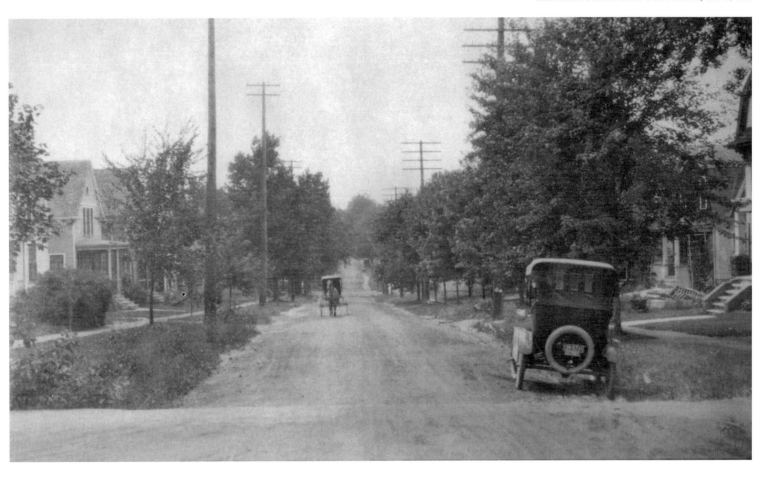

The Staebler Oil Company on State Street, ca. 1920. The first Staebler filling station was located in the old Philip Bach mansion on Main Street. Businesses offering automobile services were on the rise in the 1920s. At the start of the decade, Ann Arbor had 15 garages, 9 auto repair shops, and 4 rental companies.

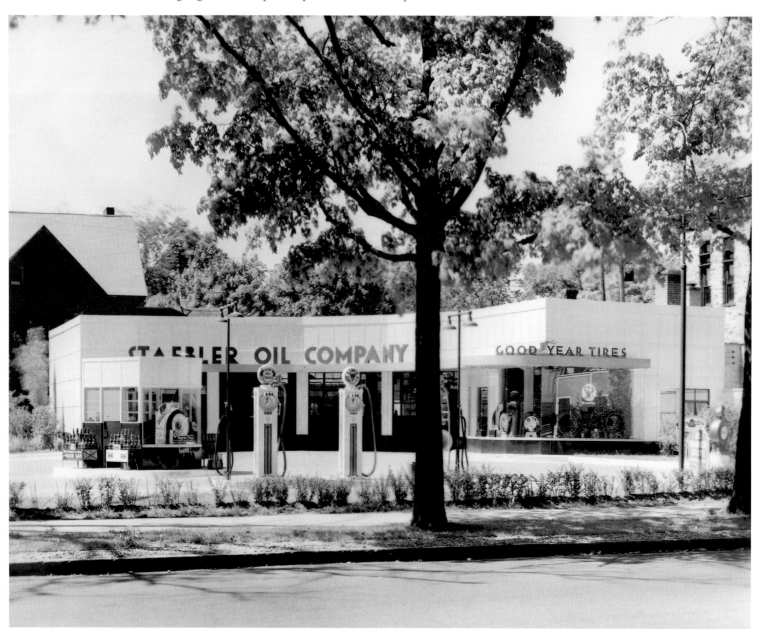

After World War I, several new churches sprang up to serve the growing community of laborers who came to work on the city's many building projects.

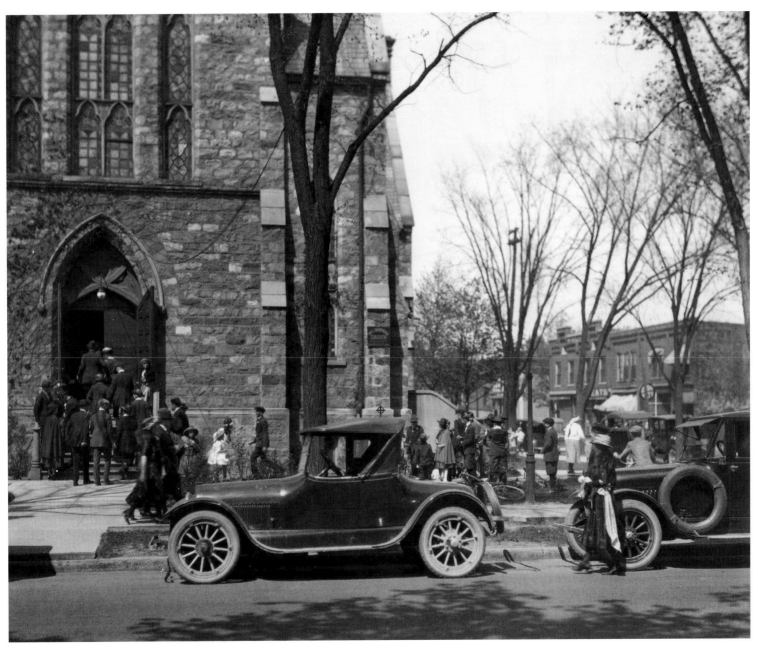

The University Museum, 1921. The building, completed in 1881, housed the University of Michigan's natural history collections until it became the Modern Languages Building in 1928. It was demolished in 1958.

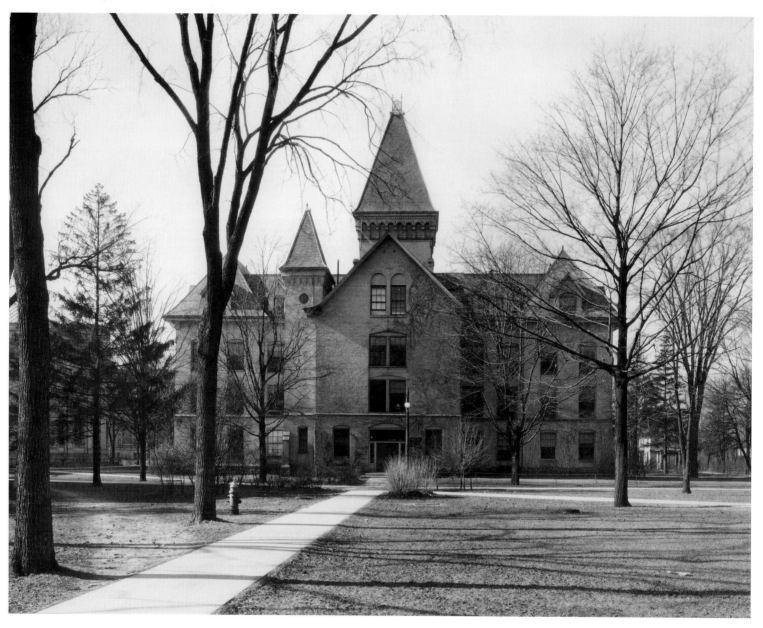

Liberty Meat Market, at 118 West Liberty Street, ca. 1920. Sullivan's Cadillac hams are advertised as "the brand to demand."

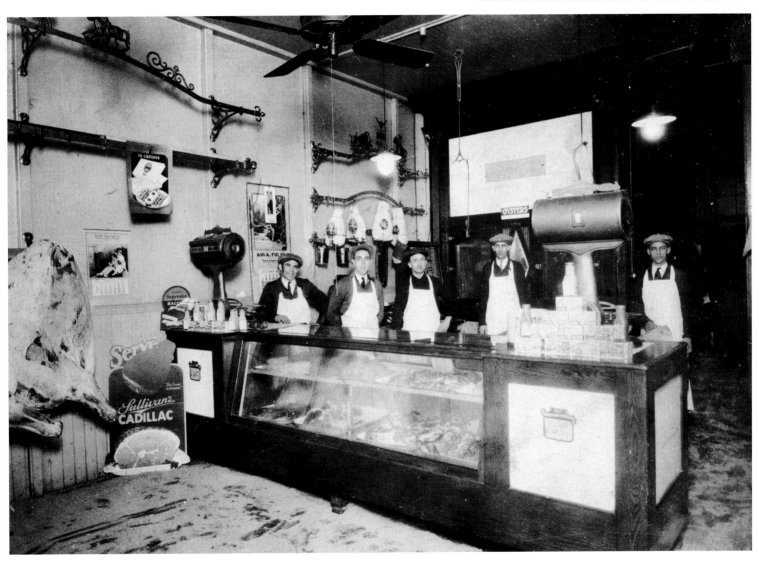

In view here is the Hoover Steel Ball Company plant, at the intersection of Hoover Street and the Ann Arbor Railway. The manufacturer of ball bearings was founded in 1913 by Leander Hoover, a businessman from Philadelphia, and became one of the biggest local industries of the early twentieth century. The main factory had 131,000 square feet of floor space and employed more than four hundred workers.

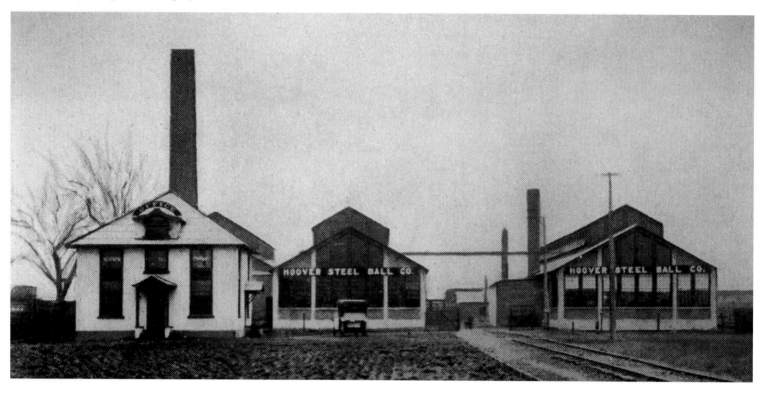

My-T-Fine Cafe, at 101-105 S. Thayer Street, ca. 1921.

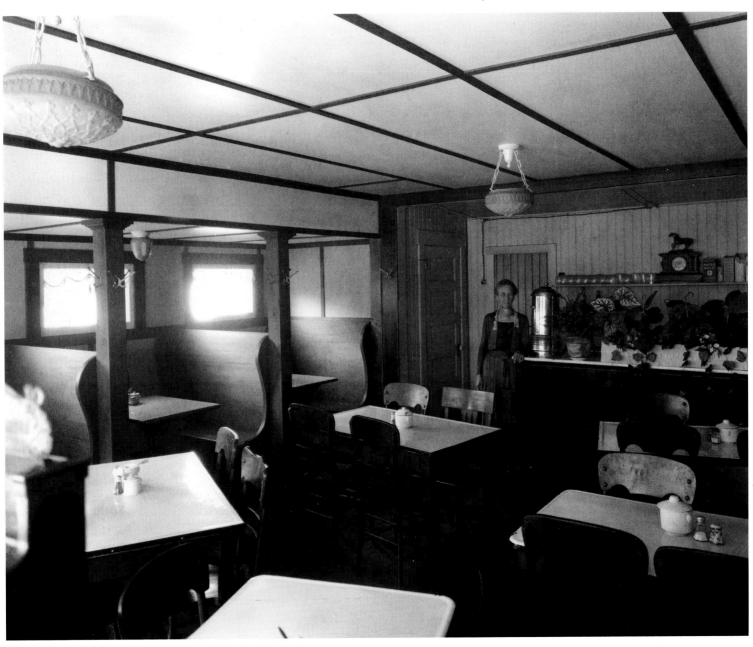

The busy shopping district of State Street, shown here in the 1920s.

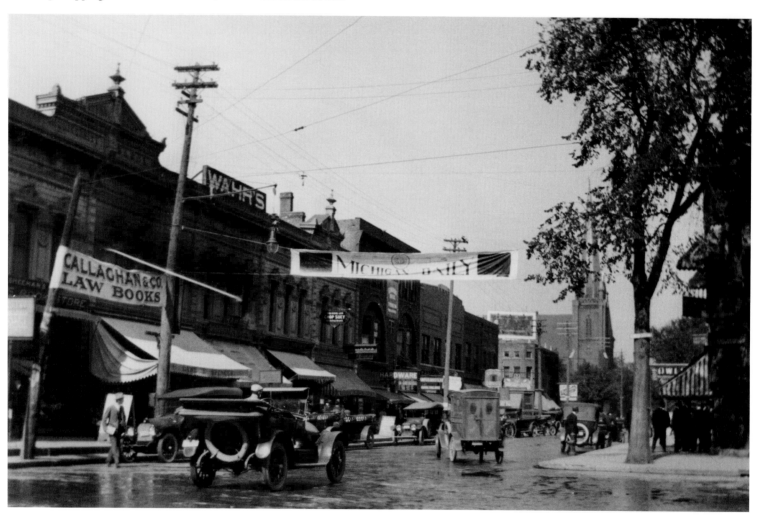

Staebler & Sons was a prominent name in the Ann Arbor automobile business. Staebler started out in 1885 as a purveyor of bicycles and offered the first car in 1900, the Trimoto (sometimes nicknamed the "Tomato"), a three-wheeled vehicle made by the American Bicycle Company of Chicago. By the 1930s Staebler had switched completely to automobiles. Pictured is their showroom at 119 West Washington Street, ca. 1930.

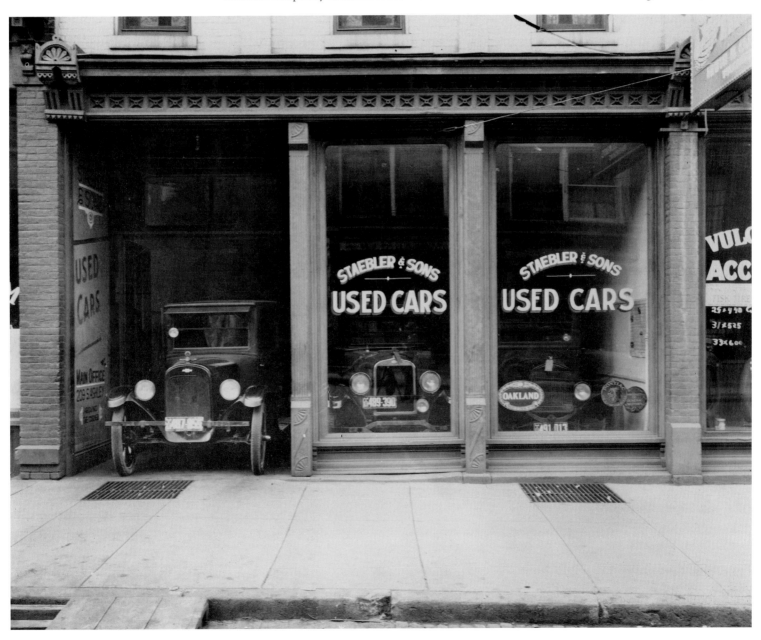

The Bethlehem Church of Christ served an almost exclusively German immigrant community in Ann Arbor well into the twentieth century. Until 1916 services were conducted only in German. Gradually the church began to offer services in English, and by 1922, when this group portrait was made, even the parish school had begun to teach pupils in English. The sanctuary dates from 1895. Designed by Rasemann, an architect out of Detroit, it was built for a sum of $20,000.

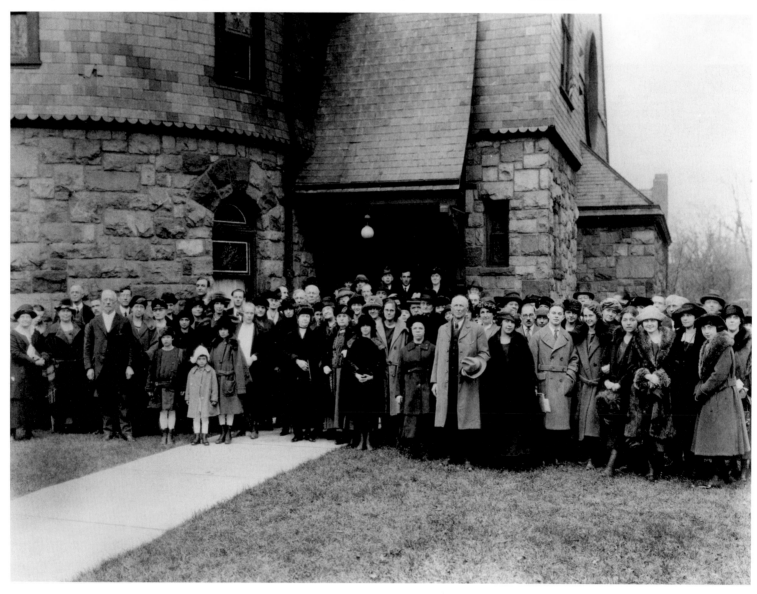

The local electric trolley system had been a staple of public transportation in Ann Arbor and greater Washtenaw County for many years. In 1925, trolleys were replaced with buses, extending service to a larger area than was possible by rail. In this photograph, the old trolleys are ushered out of town by a line of new incoming city buses.

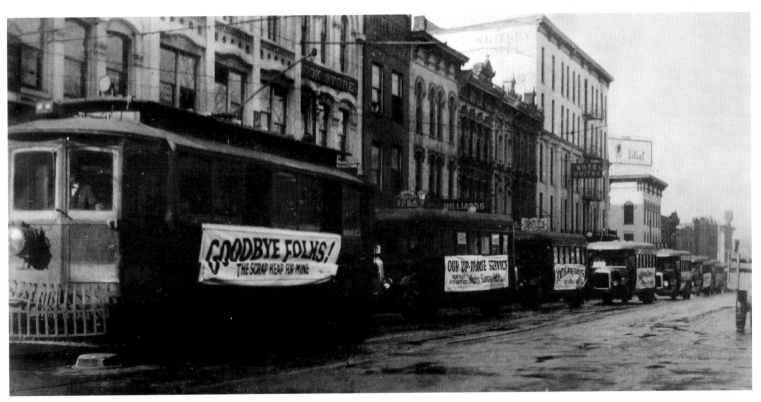

Main Street in the 1920s. As car ownership increased, Ann Arbor became a city crowded with traffic. Such was the car craze that in 1927, University of Michigan president Burton, along with the Board of Regents, declared that no student was permitted to operate a car, except in unusual circumstances, and at the discretion of the dean of students. At left in the photograph, Grinnell Bros. advertises pianos and Victrolas.

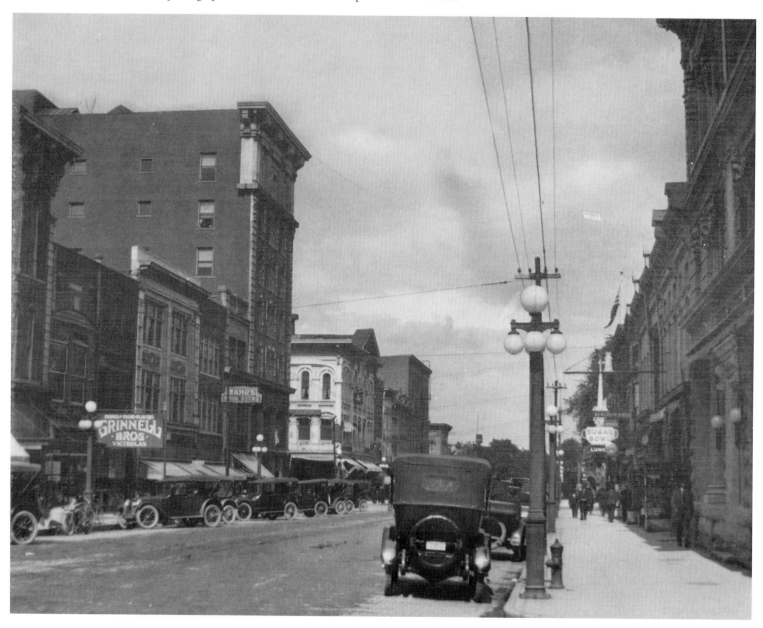

Firemen climb the tower of the fire station on the corner of Huron and 5th Avenue. The growth of the fire department followed the rapid expansion of the city during the mid 1920s. By 1925, the department boasted two pump trucks, two service trucks, one hook-and-ladder truck, a chief's car, and a platoon of 30 men.

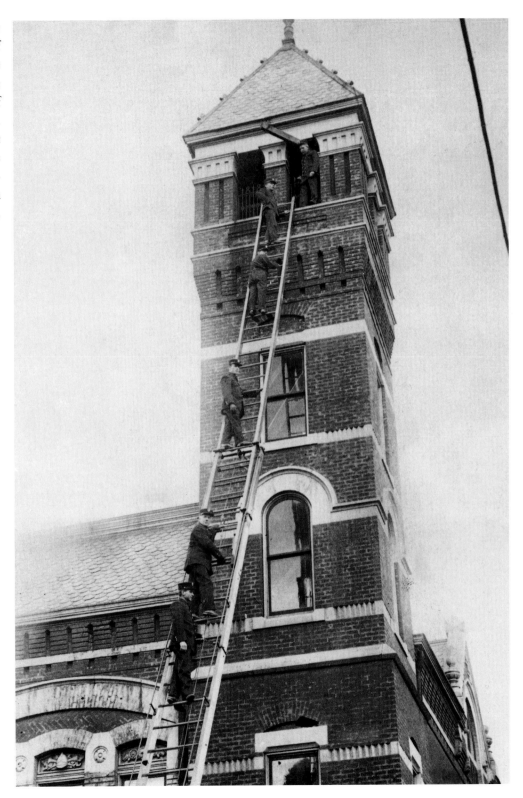

On the corner of Main and Huron streets stands the Ann Arbor Savings Bank, founded in 1869. A venerated local institution, it was the largest bank in the city in the mid 1920s. The bank maintained a branch on North University Avenue.

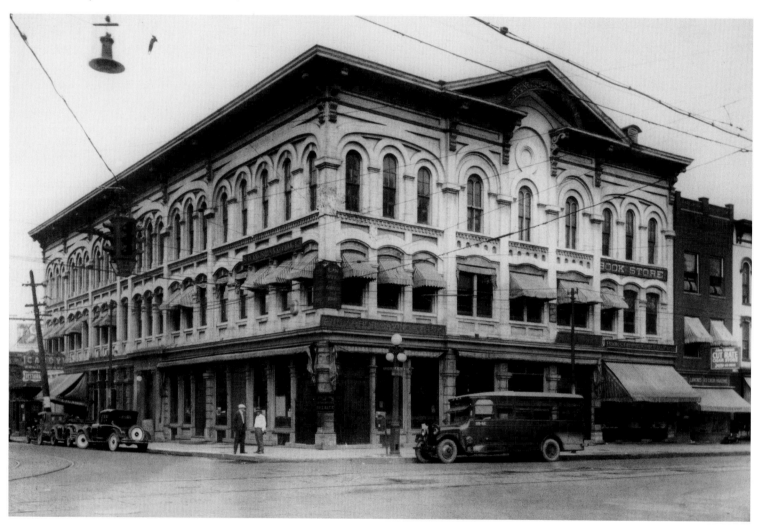

In August 1927, diners at Prochnow's Dairy Lunch on Main Street were rattled from their meals by a spectacular crash. Four cars from the Interurban train had slipped their couplings and rolled down the tracks into town, finally derailing and smashing into the Farmers and Mechanics Bank. The building sustained great damage, but miraculously, no one was injured.

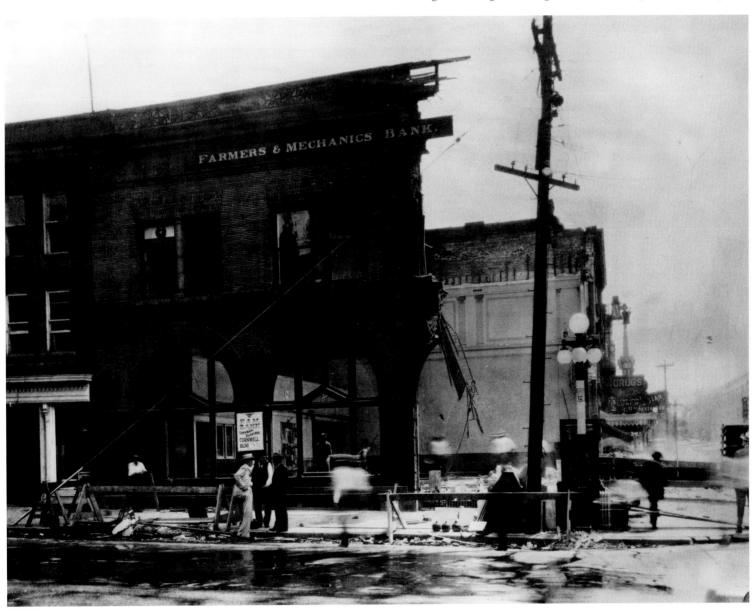

The Varsity Laundry Company, founded by Fred Lantz, Clarence Snyder, and H. B. Tenny, was yet another local company to embrace the automobile. In 1913, Varsity retired its horse-drawn delivery carriages in favor of new Dodge delivery trucks.

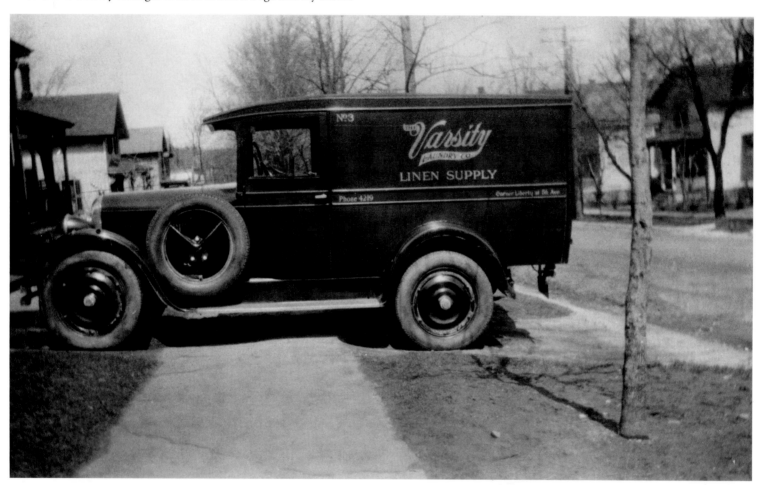

Pontiac Trail, at the corner of Cedar Lane. The 1866 Methodist church is visible in the distance.

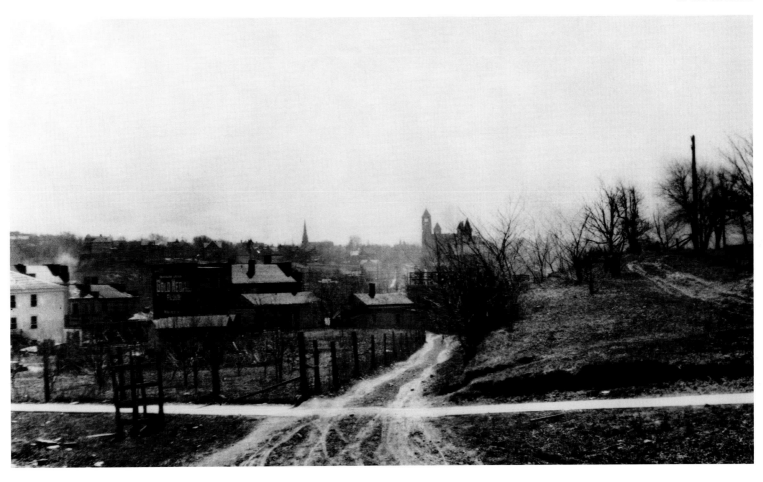

Pontiac Trail, in Lower Town, ca. 1922, surrounded by small farms. The trail, as seen from the Detroit Edison's Argo substation, was still very rural at this time.

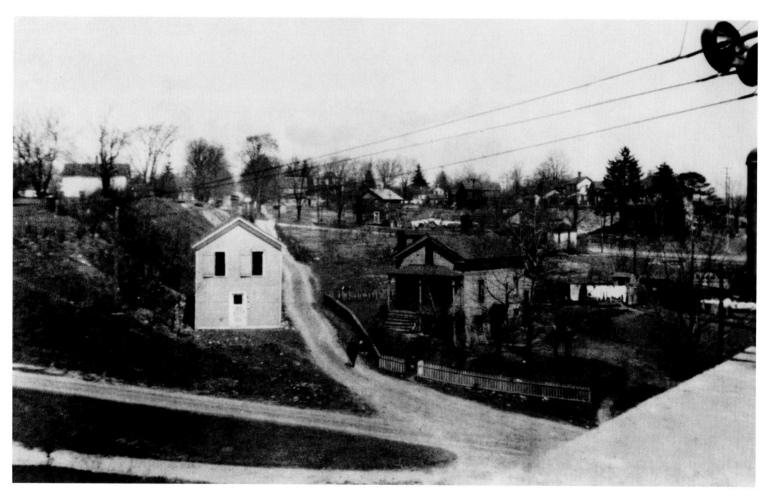

The *Ann Arbor Daily News* building, in 1936.

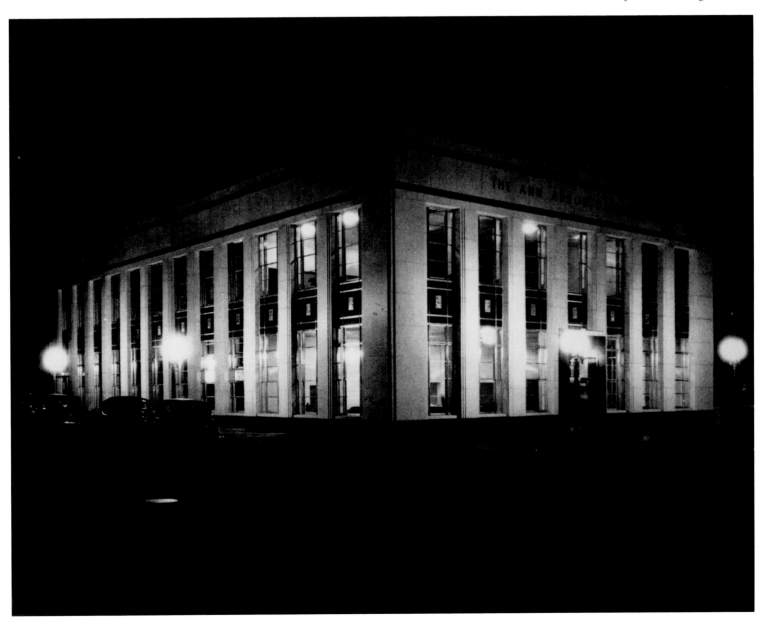

Ice cream cones are available for 5¢ at the concession stand at Island Drive Park. The park was one of several in Ann Arbor proposed and developed by George Burns, a professor of botany at the University of Michigan. Located behind Michigan Central Station along the Huron River, the park was a popular recreation area for residents looking for a cool retreat from town.

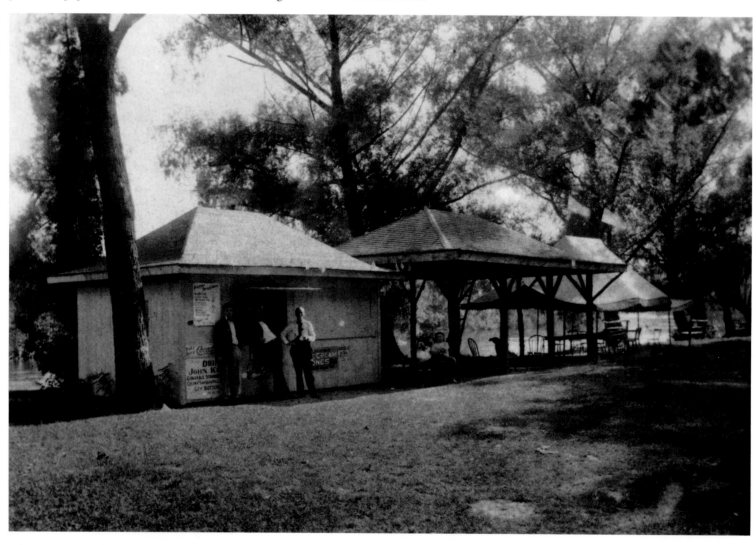

The Ann Arbor Community Orchestra was founded in 1928 by four musicians from the Ann Arbor Methodist Church. Originally the group could boast a saxophone, cornet, trombone, and piano, but it eventually grew into this substantial collective. The orchestra is in concert in March 1934, presenting works by Sousa, Romberg, and Luigini.

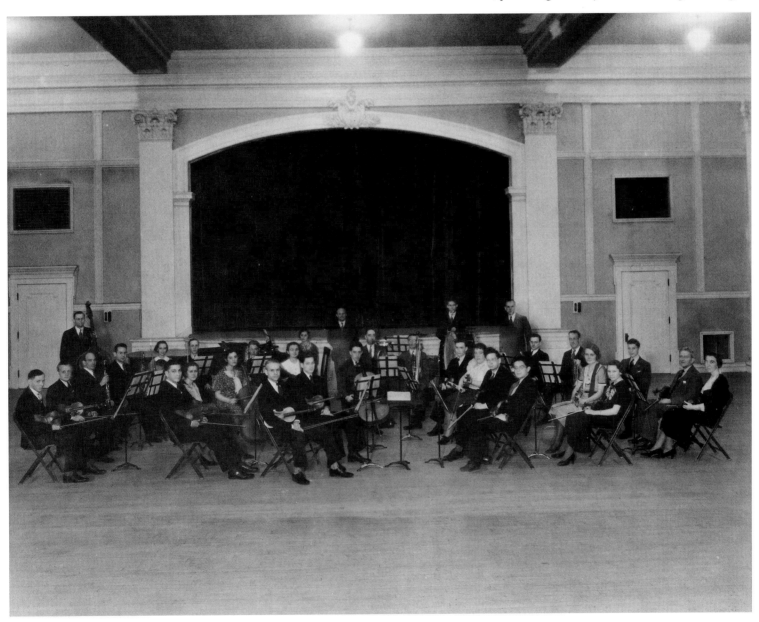

Interior of a men's clothing store, in 1932. Ties and bowties are *in.*

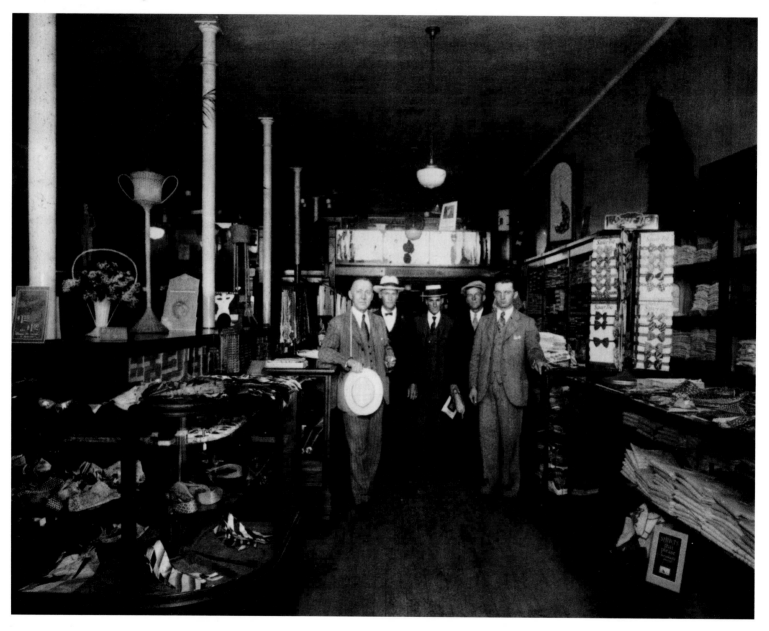

Two company vehicles advertise Drake's Sandwich Shop, at
820 East University Avenue.

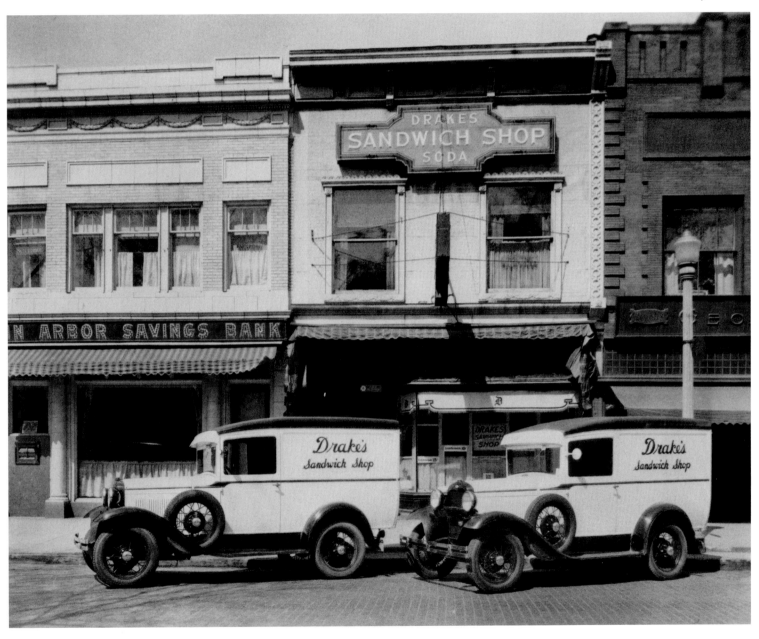

Business is under way on Maynard and Liberty in 1935. In view are Miller's Ice Cream, Collins Women's Apparel, the Craft Press, Jacobson's Women's Wear, and the University Flower Shop.

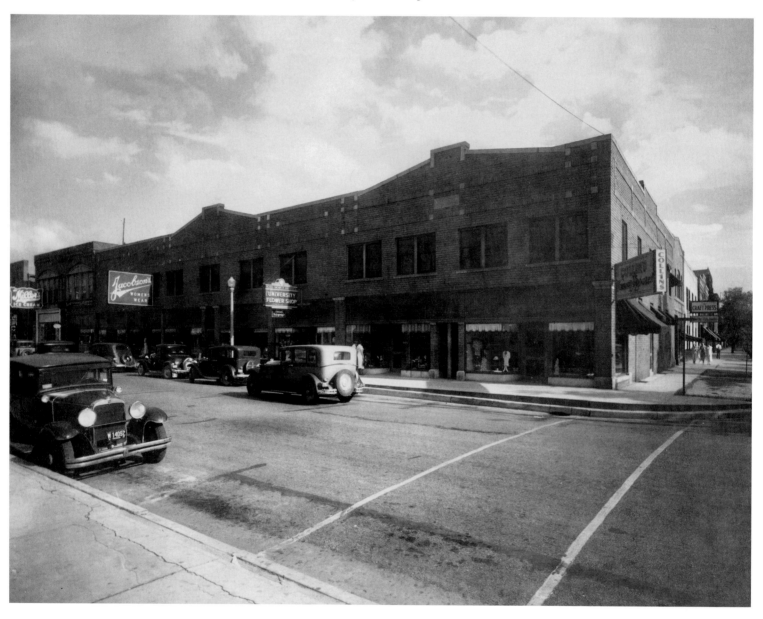

Lindenschmitt, Apfel & Company, Clothiers, Hatters and Furnishers, at 209 South Main Street, in 1934.

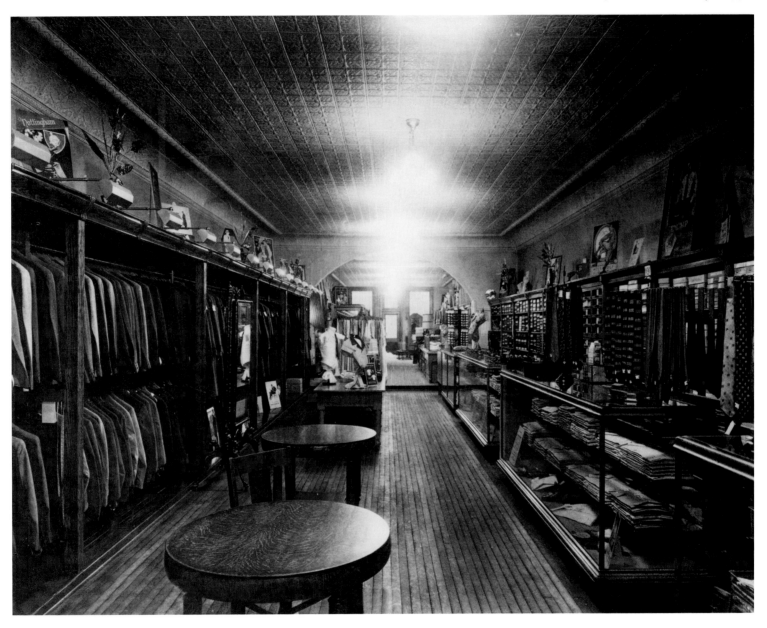

The Staebler Oil Company showroom, in 1933.

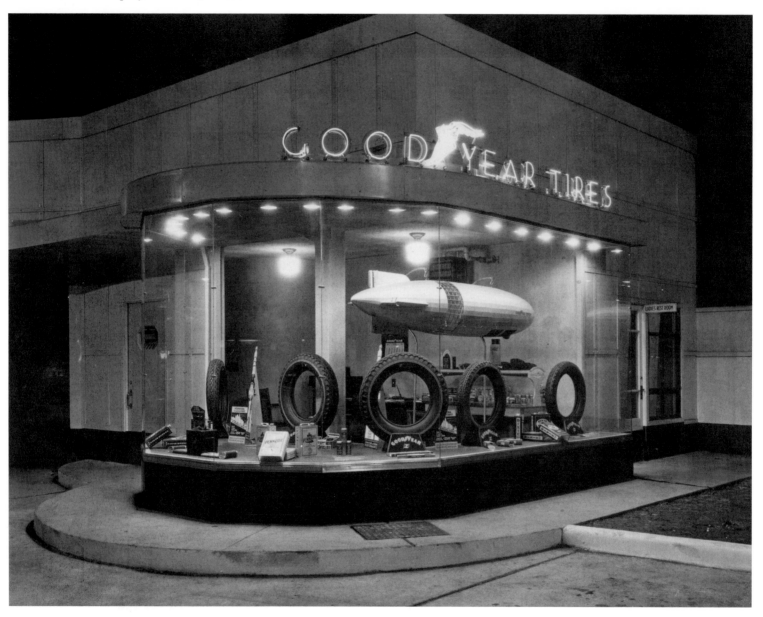

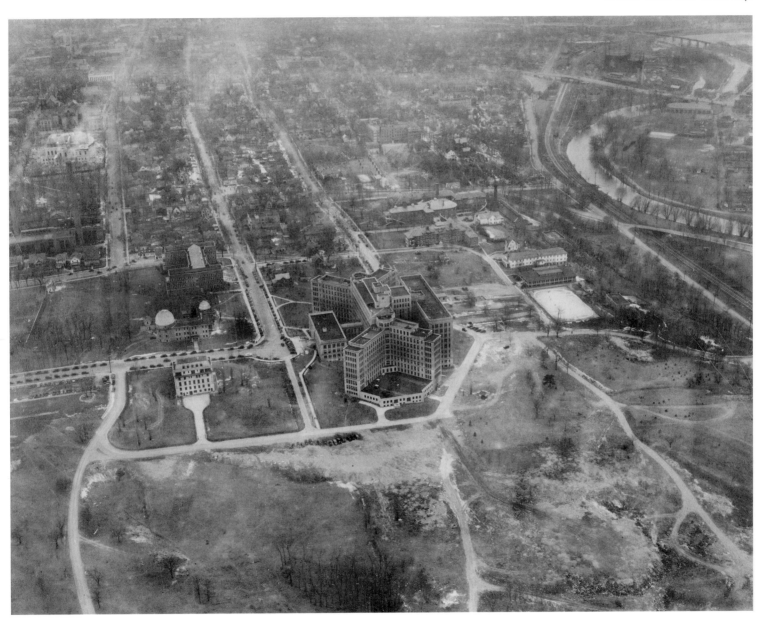

A 1937 aerial view of the city.

Main and Packard streets, in 1937, where an automobile
garage offers "fine service for fine cars."

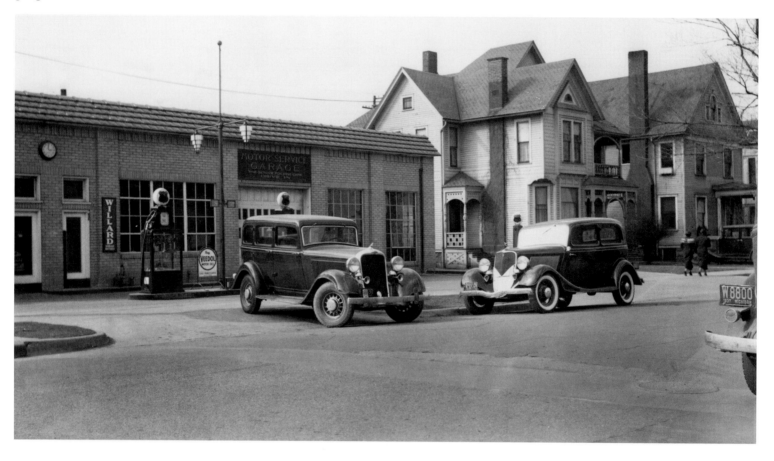

Quarry Drug Store on North University and South State Street. A sign to the left says "New Location For Moe's Barber Shop." The building is now home to the Michigan Book and Supply Store.

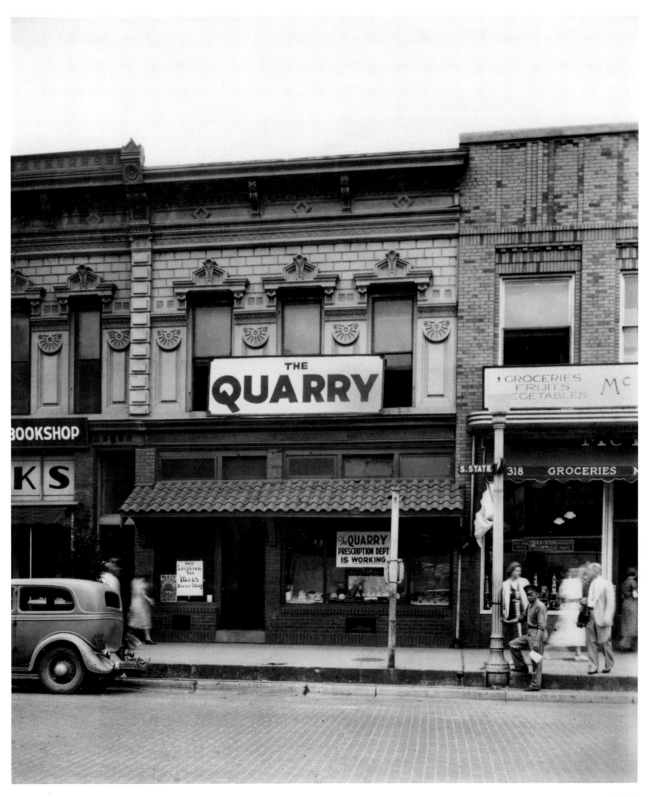

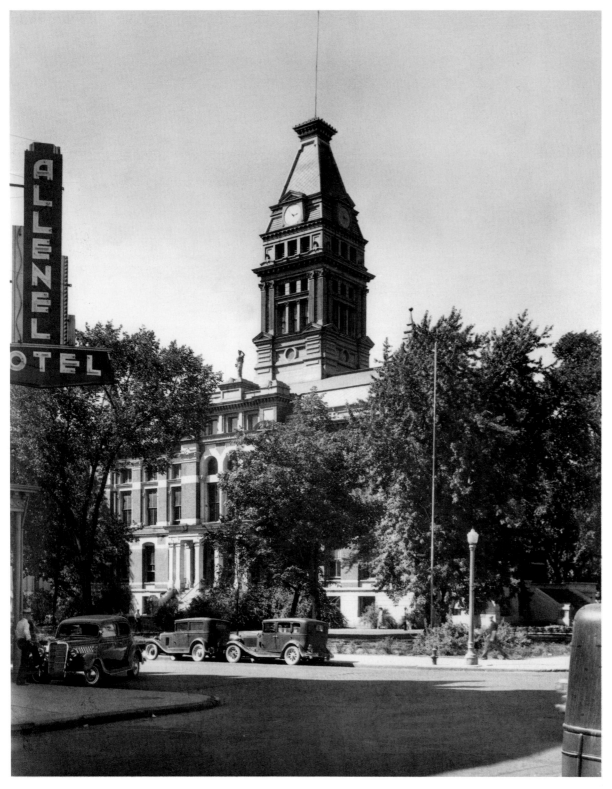

The Washtenaw County Courthouse, at Main and Huron streets. Many of the aerial photographs of the city were taken from the tower of this building. The cornerstone for the building was laid in 1877. To the left, a taxicab is parked in front of the Allenel Hotel.

The Cornwell Coal Co., at Huron Street and 4th Avenue. Cornwell's occupied the Hamilton Block, built in 1882. Before Cornwell moved in, the building housed the Postal Telegraph Company and a bowling alley.

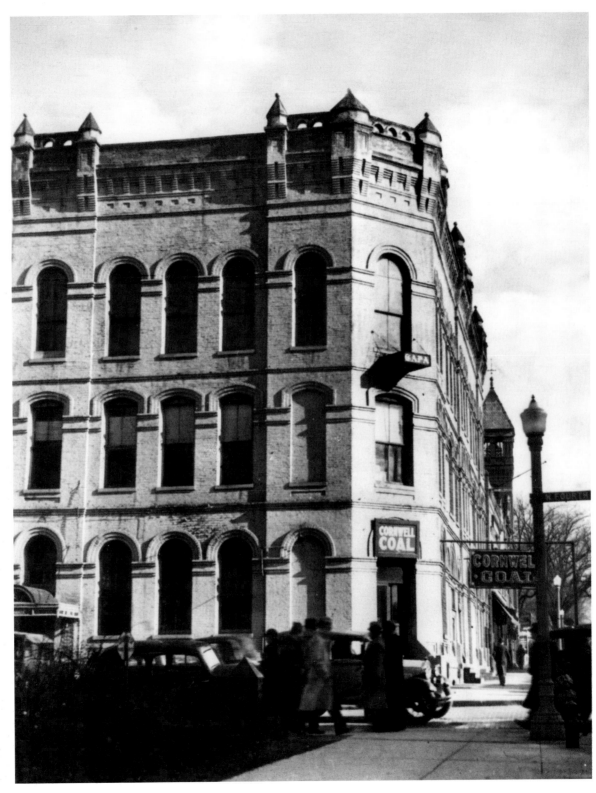

Through the WPA, many different public works facilities were built in Ann Arbor during the Great Depression. Here, WPA workers construct a band shell in West Park. The band shell still stands and continues to be a popular summer venue for concerts and other events.

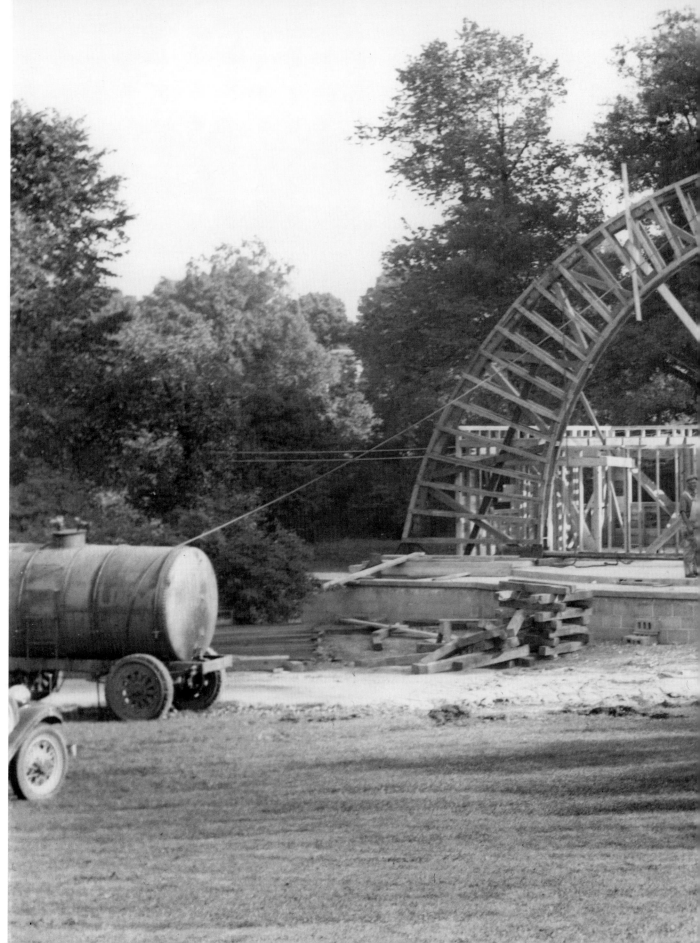

178

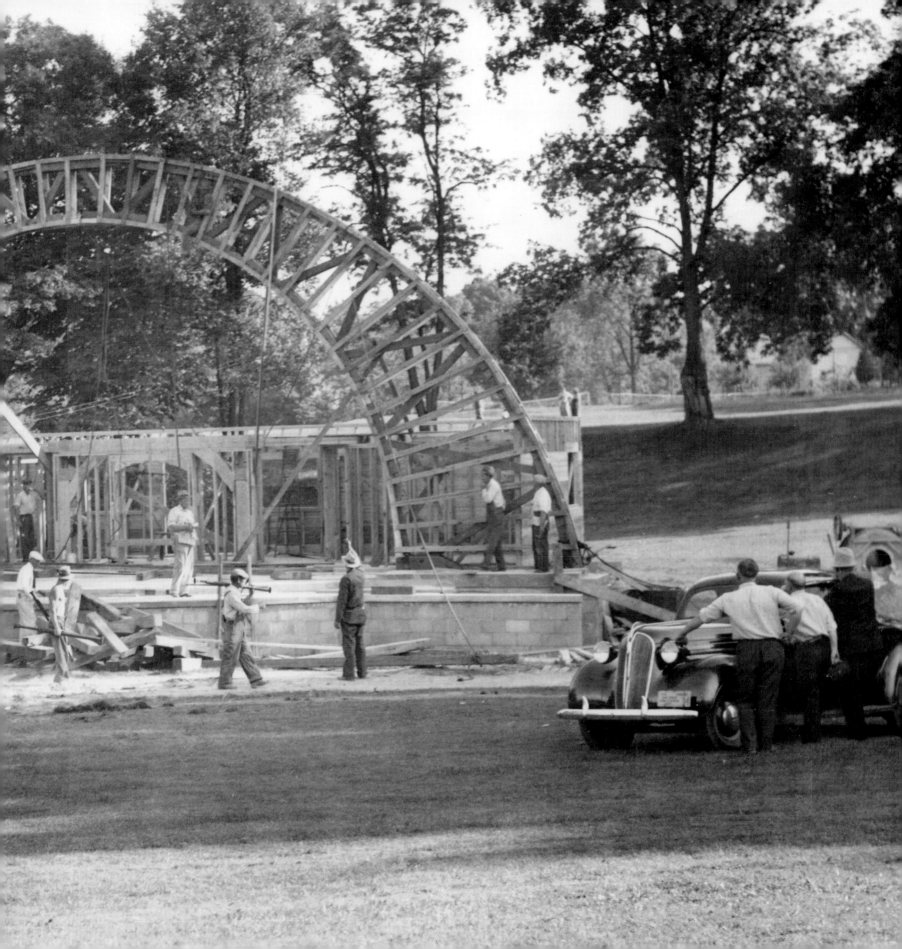

The Quarry Drugstore. Upstairs, the Laura Belle
Shop is holding a sale.

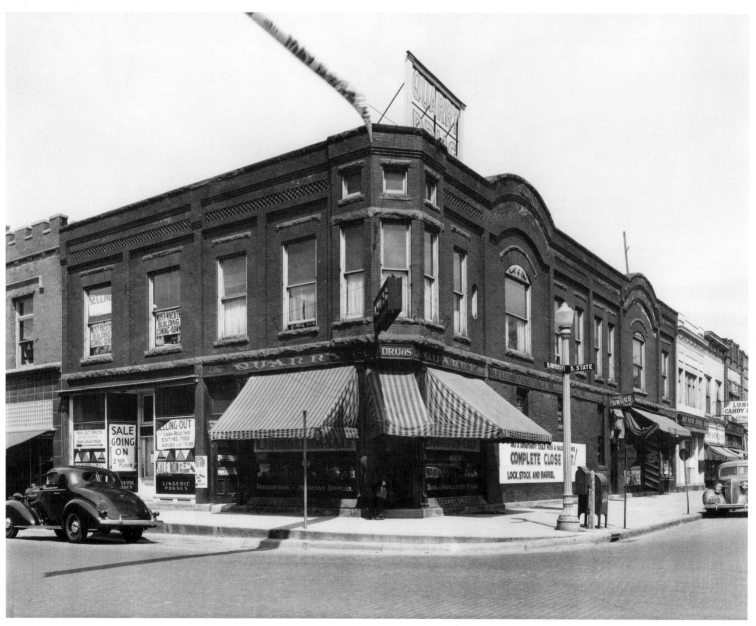

State Street on an evening in 1933.

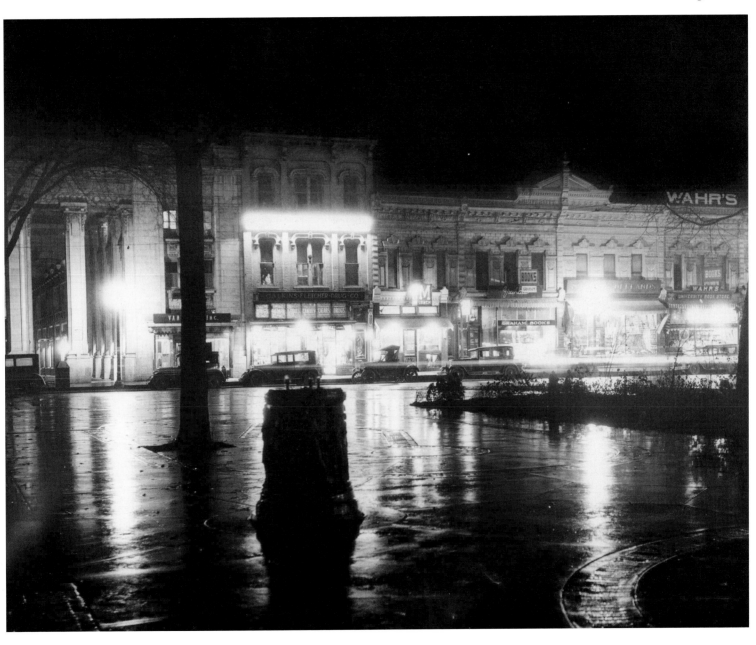

Murray Avenue, in Ann Arbor's Westside.

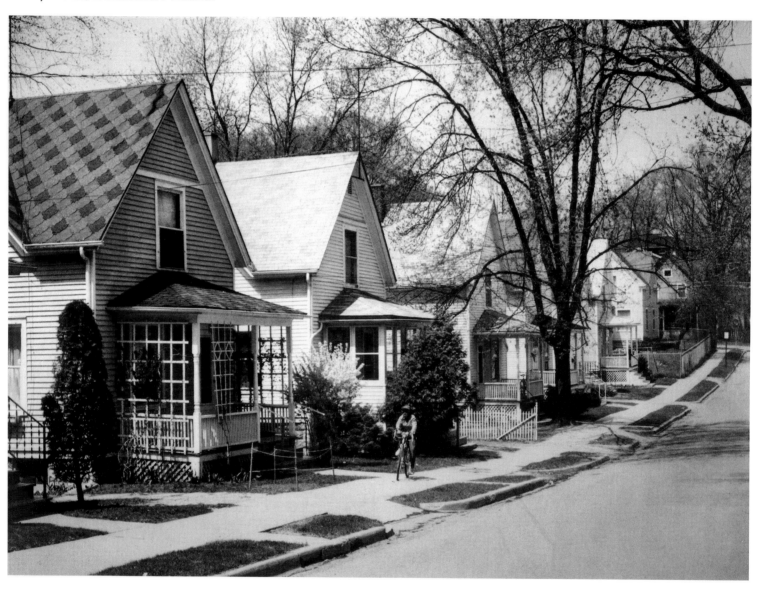

ON THE NATIONAL STAGE

(1940–1960s)

As the United States entered World War II in 1941, Ann Arbor once again answered the call to duty as industry retooled to contribute to the war effort. Area firms such as the King-Seeley Company, which had expanded greatly in the previous decade, began producing machine parts for the military, and the Willow Run Airport, in nearby Ypsilanti, began building B-24 aircraft. The Argus Company, manufacturer of the popular Argus point-and-shoot camera, turned its production lines to the manufacture of telescopes and radio equipment for the armed forces. Like many American towns in this period, wartime industry fueled growth and brought prosperity to a society still recovering from the Great Depression.

By the end of World War II, Ann Arbor had transformed from a small midwestern hamlet in the early nineteenth century to a booming epicenter for commerce and research. Owing in part to the increasingly high profile of the University of Michigan, it was clearly a town with a place in the national consciousness. Ann Arbor served as the stage for many events that drew national attention. The development, testing, and final release of the Salk polio vaccine in 1955 at the university's School of Public Health was a widely heralded breakthrough. Reporting on the event, the *New York Times* noted that "a mass invasion of newsmen and scientists [have] turned this usually quiet University of Michigan town into a beehive of suspense and speculation." In the early 1950s, Ann Arbor became home to one of the nation's first digital computers. The Michigan Digital Automatic Computer (MIDAC) was built at the university's Willow Run Laboratories under government contract.

The city also played host to prominent political figures of the period. During the 1952 presidential campaign, candidate Adlai Stevenson visited town, followed shortly after by then vice-presidential hopeful Richard Nixon. In 1960, John F. Kennedy spoke from the steps of the university's Michigan Union, and Richard Nixon returned, this time as a presidential candidate, to speak at the Michigan Central Depot. Ann Arbor had become a nexus of people and ideas that would only grow stronger as the city continued to forge its identity on the national stage.

Ann Arbor has always received its fair share of snow, as depicted here around 1940.

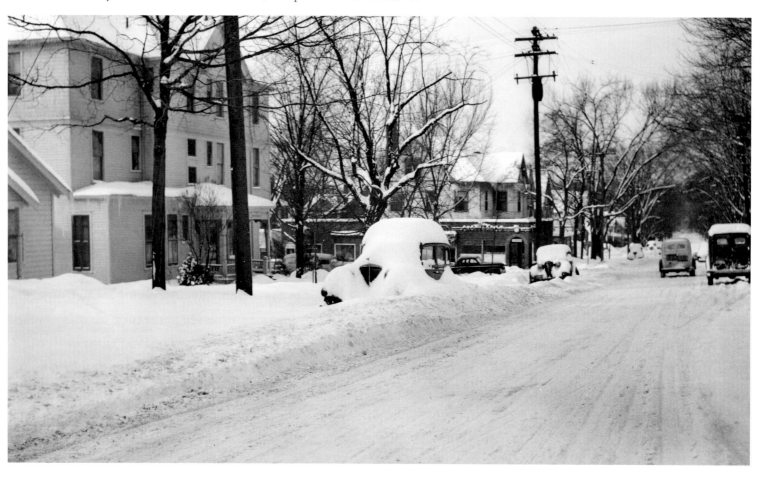

With winter weather comes the need for snow removal. During the 1930s, most snow was still removed with horse-drawn plow. By the 1940s, trucks and other motorized equipment were handling the task.

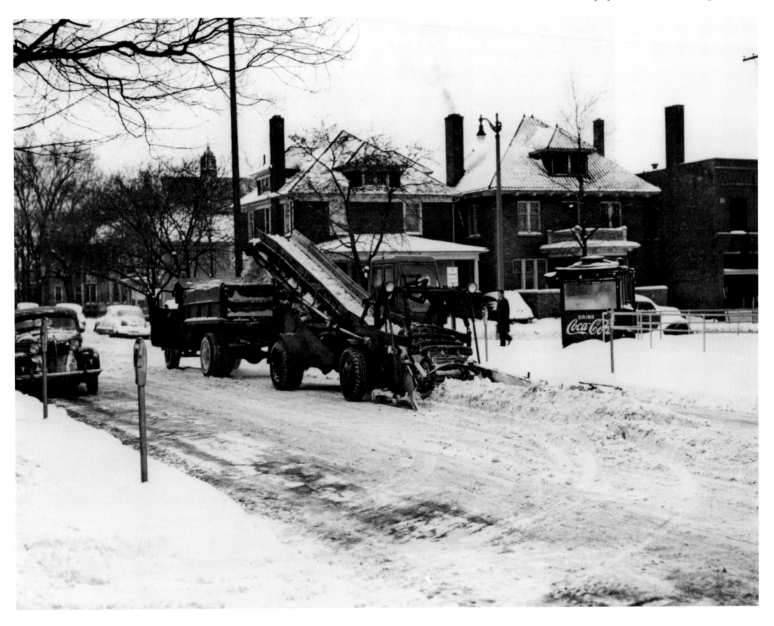

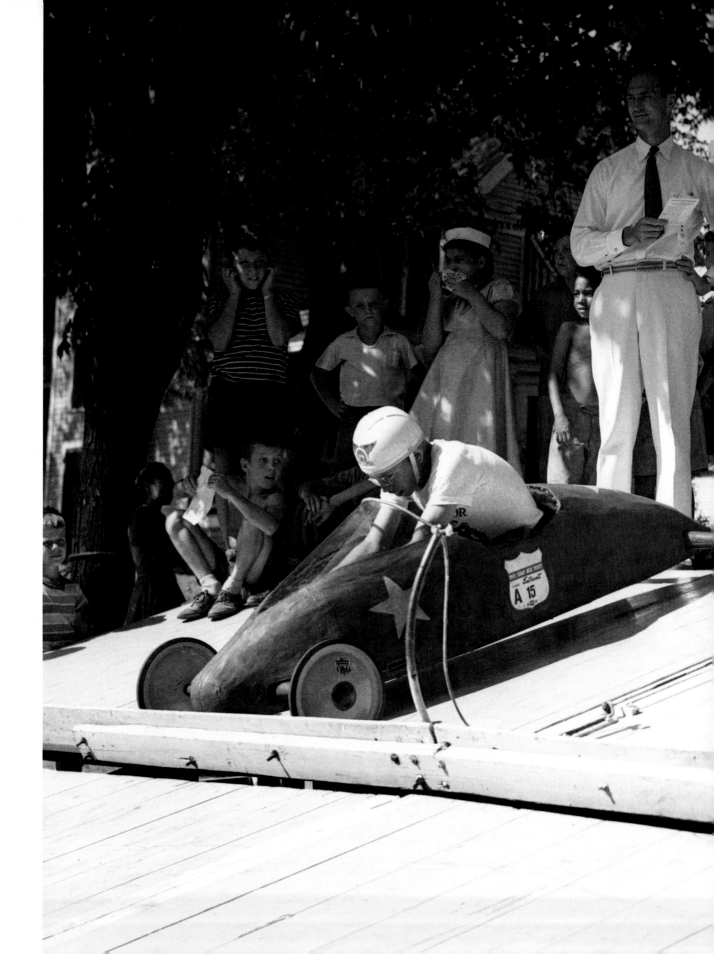

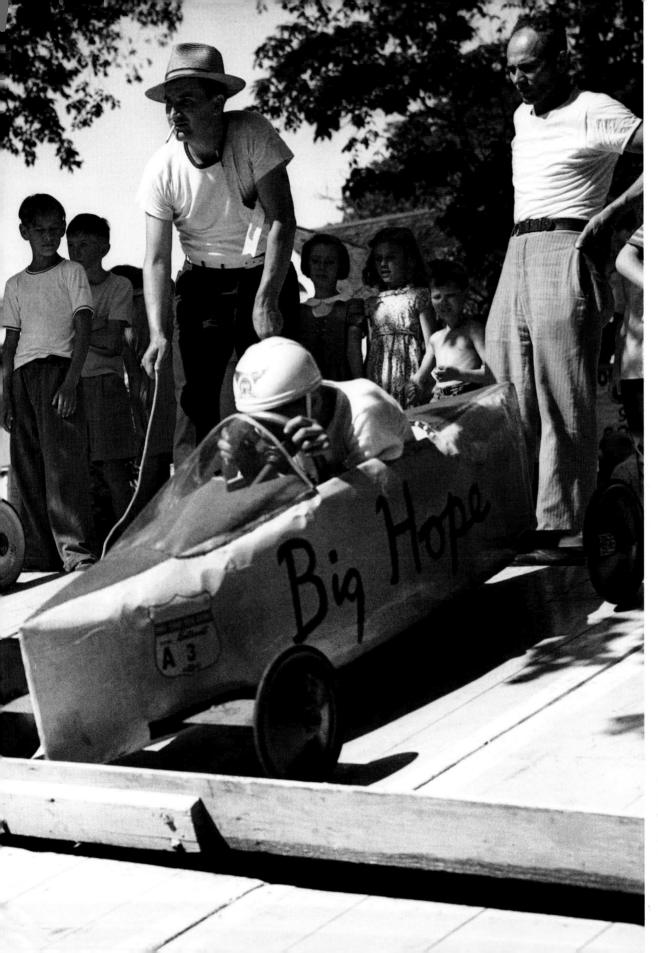

Soap Box Derbies were popular entertainment, and were sponsored by local groups, such as the Junior Chamber of Commerce.

187

The King-Seeley Company was a prominent manufacturer of automotive parts. During World War II, the company was among the city's chief producers of machine parts for the military, with contracts to produce fuse and torpedo parts for the Navy, air valves and eliminators for the Air Corps, and fin assemblies for the Army.

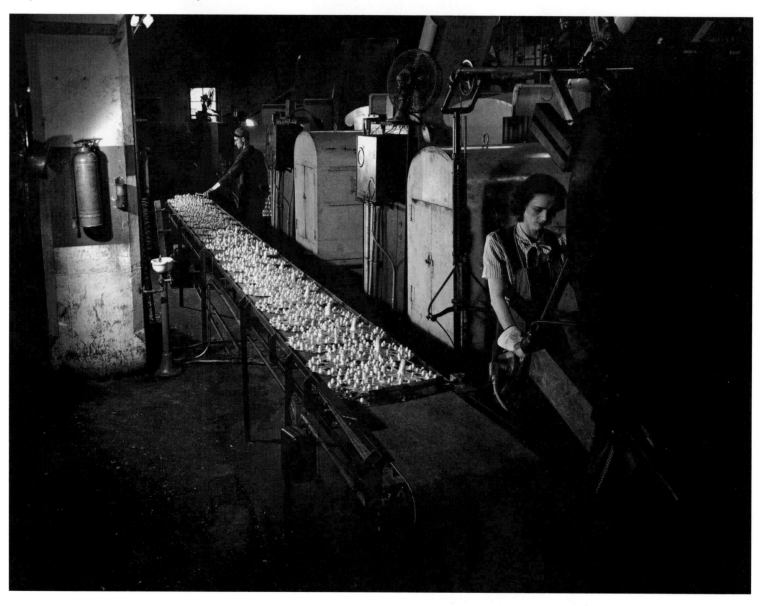

The original caption for this photograph states: "Prof. George Ross of the University Landscape Architectural Department enjoy[s] a quiet smoke as he gaze[s] with satisfaction at the amazing beauty of the flower show, which was the realization of his dreams come true through the designs he created. Beyond him is the popular police sergeant 'Red' Howard; while Mrs. Dean Loree presides at the information booth" (ca. 1940).

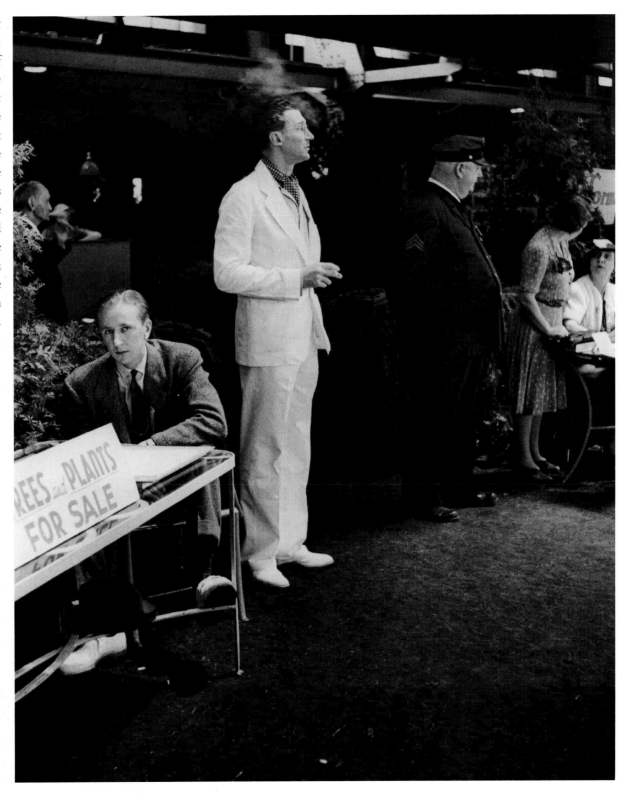

Social Services for Crippled Children, ca. 1940. The University Hospital moved in 1925 to new facilities on Ann Street, which housed special accommodations for children, including a recreation area and school.

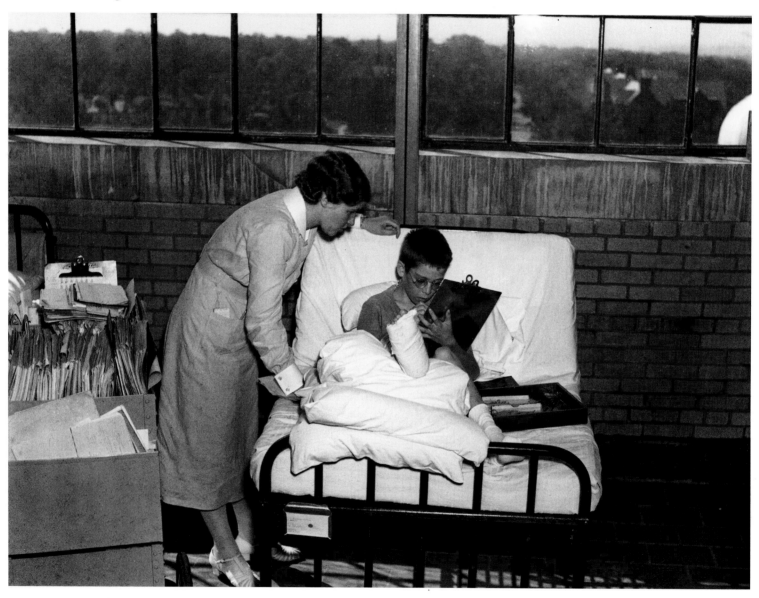

During the war, the Junior Chamber of Commerce was a central organizer of relief efforts and programs for young people. The group was founded in Ann Arbor in 1935 and by 1941 it enrolled 93 members. Although it was responsible for many different kinds of community service projects, its "War Services" branch was especially active. One hundred percent of Ann Arbor "Jaycee" members participated in war services projects in the early 1940s.

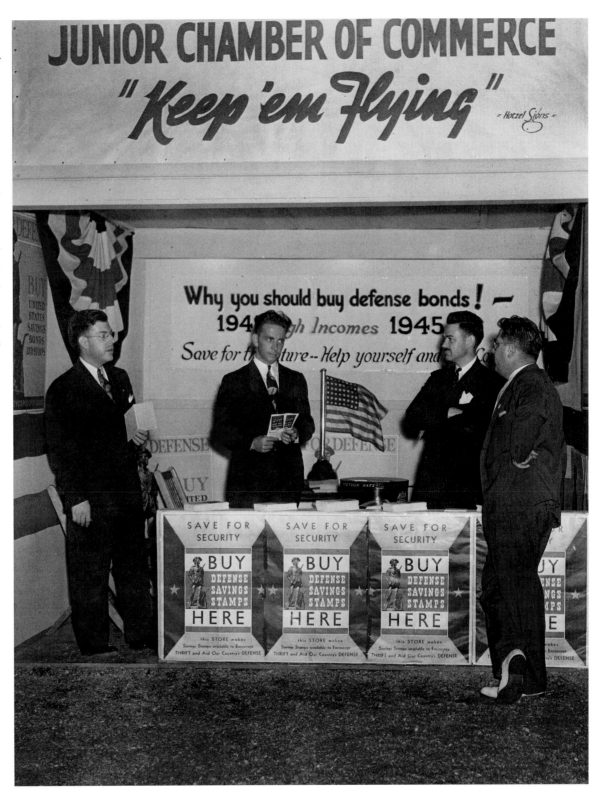

The Junior Chamber of Commerce also organized events for veterans returning from the war after 1945. Shown here is a recreation event.

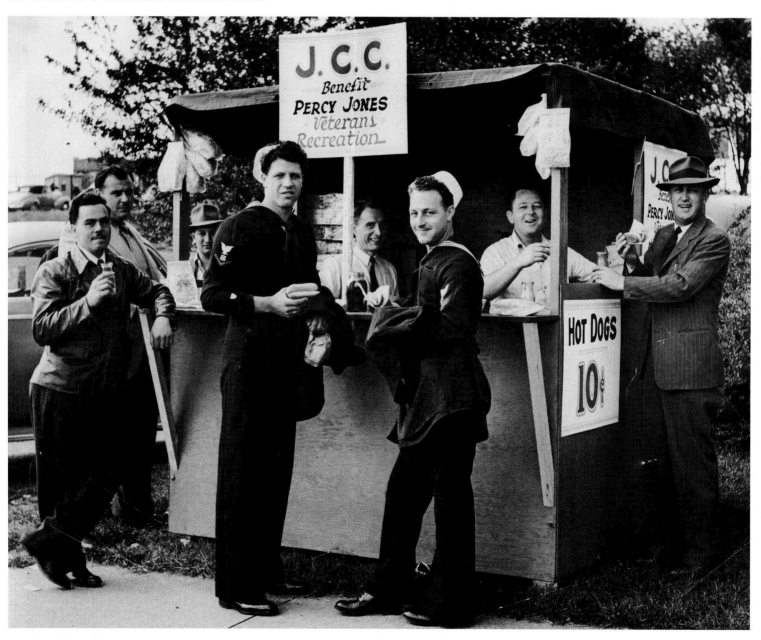

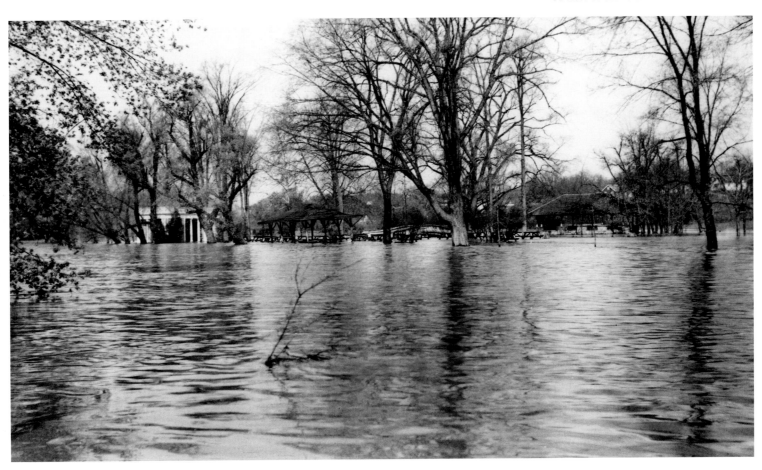

A view of the Island Park flood of 1943.

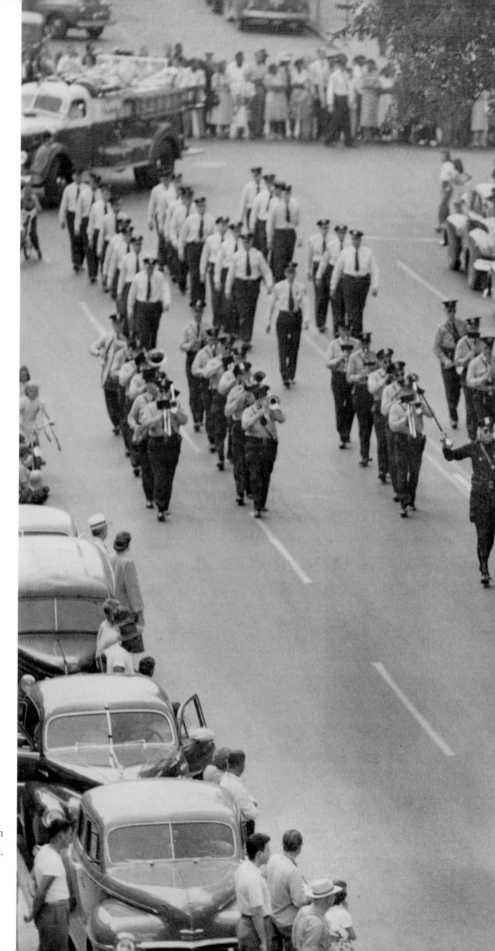

The Ann Arbor Police Band performs in a parade in celebration
of Rededication Week 1948.

194

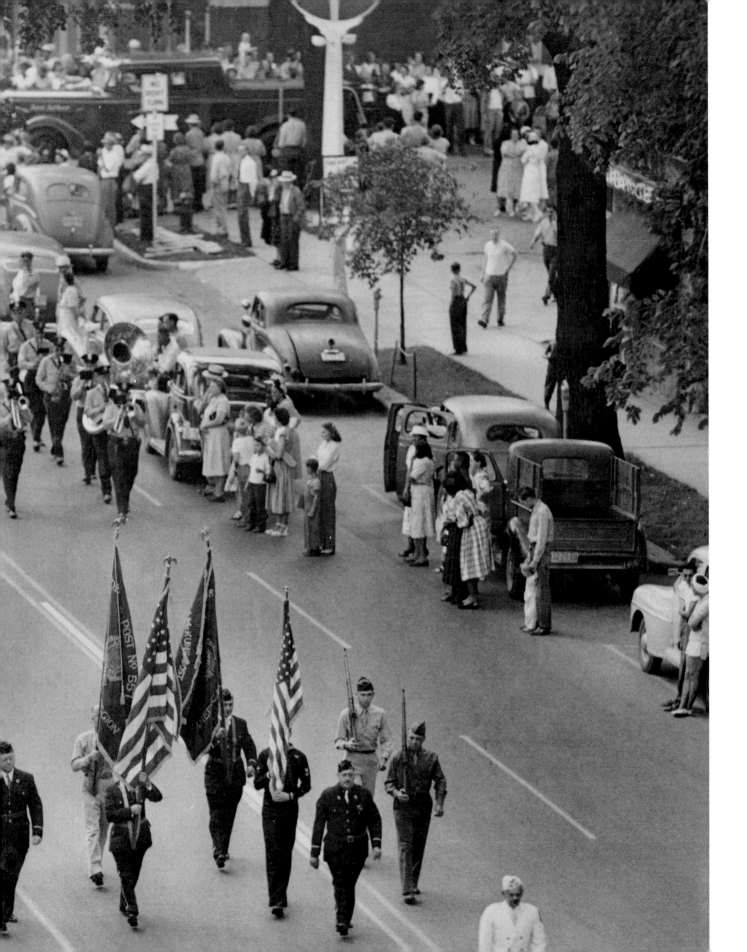

The intersection of North University and State Street.

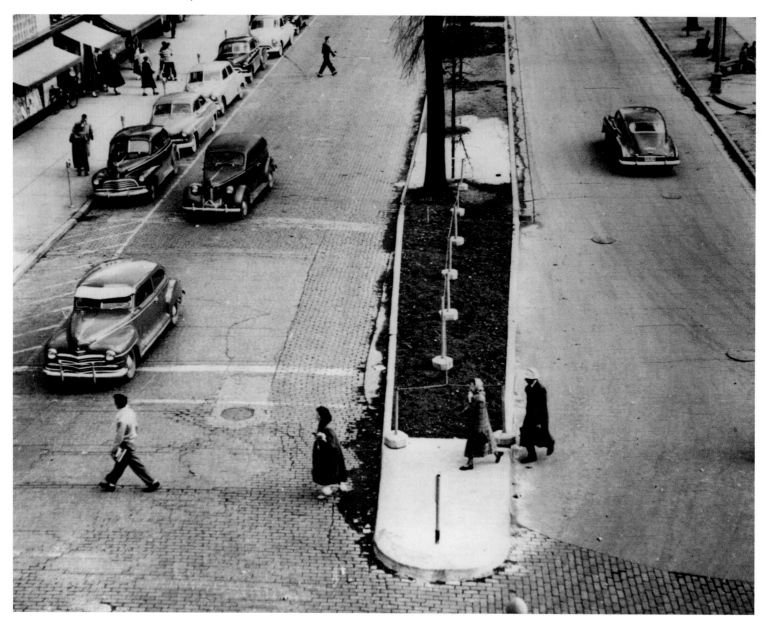

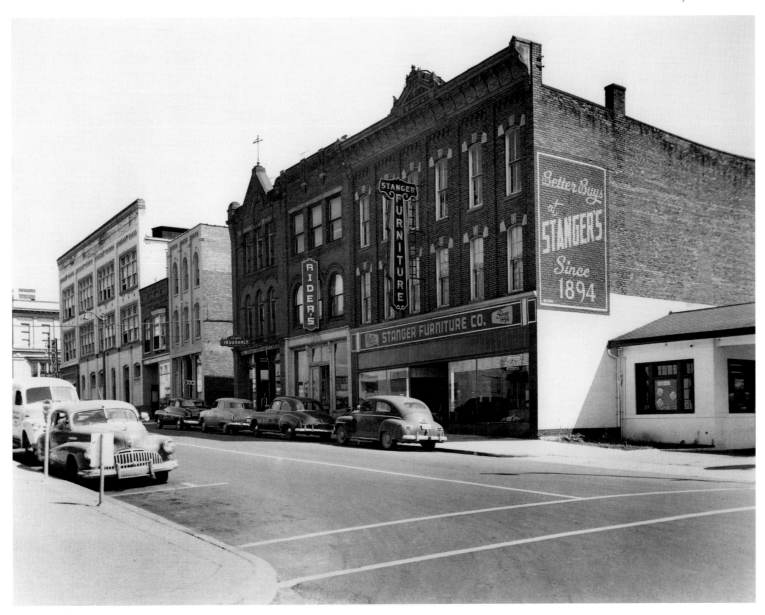

Liberty Street, 1952.

The Michigan Theater, 1949. The Michigan Theater was built in 1928 on East Liberty Street with 2,200 seats. The original marquee was replaced in 1946, and ten years later the interior was modernized. Here patrons stand in line to see the premiere of *It Happens Every Spring,* a comedy starring Ray Milland.

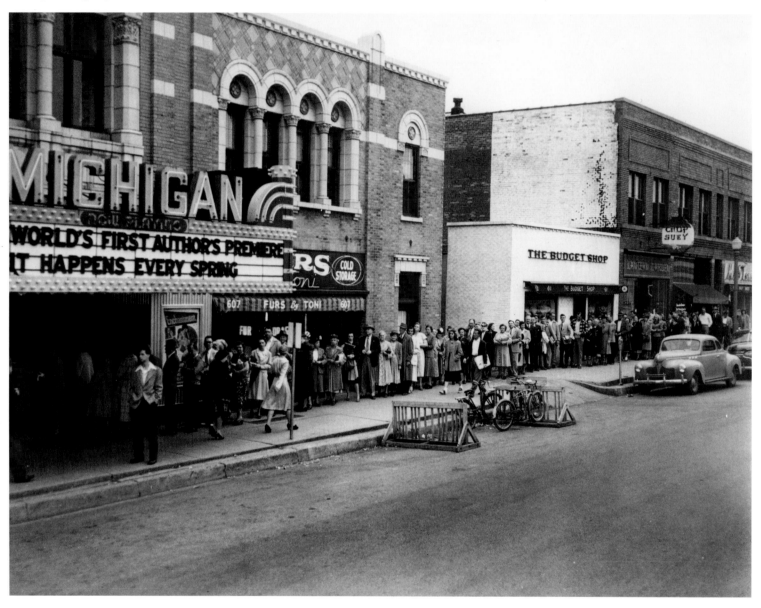

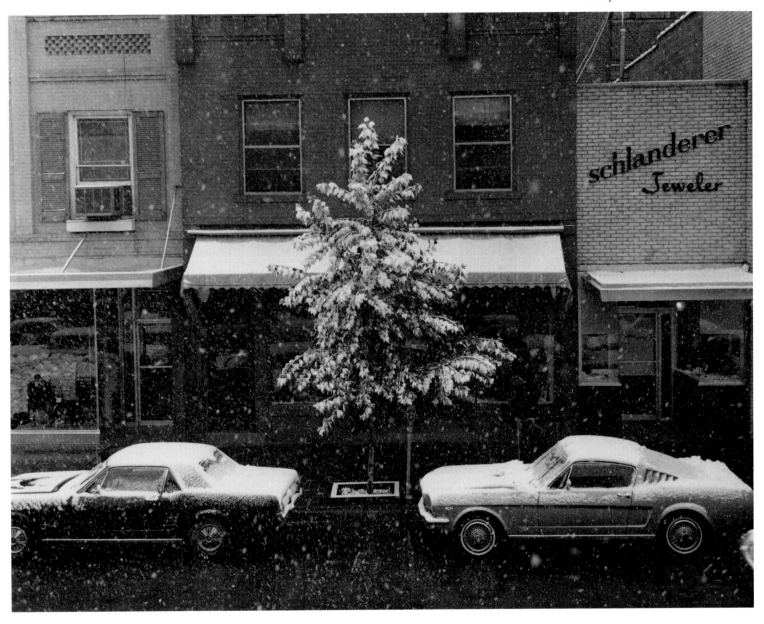

A snowy Main Street, late 1960s. Schlanderer & Sons jewelers are still in business today, at 208 South Main Street.

NOTES ON THE PHOTOGRAPHS

These notes, listed by page number, attempt to include all aspects known of the photographs. Each of the photographs is identified by the page number, photograph's title or description, photographer and collection, archive, and call or box number when applicable. Although every attempt was made to collect all available data, in some cases complete data was unavailable due to the age and condition of some of the photographs and records.

II **ANN ARBOR**
Bentley Historical Library,
University of Michigan
HS1578

VI **RECRUITING OFFICER**
Bentley Historical Library,
University of Michigan
BL001186

X **MAIN STREET**
Bentley Historical Library,
University of Michigan
BL000821

2 **CIVIL WAR BEGINS**
Bentley Historical Library,
University of Michigan
HS1580

3 **STUDENT SOLDIERS**
Bentley Historical Library,
University of Michigan
BL003711

4 **HANGSTERFER BLOCK**
Bentley Historical Library,
University of Michigan
BL000817

5 **GREGORY HOUSE**
Bentley Historical Library,
University of Michigan
BL000823

6 **BASEBALL CLUB**
Bentley Historical Library,
University of Michigan
BL000906

7 **MAIN STREET**
Bentley Historical Library,
University of Michigan
BL000919

8 **STATE STREET**
Bentley Historical Library,
University of Michigan
BL000903

9 **FIRST PRESBYTERIAN**
Bentley Historical Library,
University of Michigan
HS1675

10 **ANN STREET**
Bentley Historical Library,
University of Michigan
BL000335

11 **FIRE DEPARTMENT**
Bentley Historical Library,
University of Michigan
HS1660

12 **DRAKE'S SALOON**
Bentley Historical Library,
University of Michigan
BL000909

13 **METHODIST CHURCH**
Bentley Historical Library,
University of Michigan
BL000281

14 **HURON RIVER**
Bentley Historical Library,
University of Michigan
HS1600

15 **BEER DELIVERY WAGON**
Bentley Historical Library,
University of Michigan
BL000902

16 **MEAT MARKET**
Bentley Historical Library,
University of Michigan
HS1596

17 **FIRST GERMAN CHURCH**
Bentley Historical Library,
University of Michigan
BL000317

18 **NORTHWEST ANN ARBOR**
Bentley Historical Library,
University of Michigan
BL000017

19 **ORGAN WORKS**
Bentley Historical Library,
University of Michigan
BL000302

20 **RAILROAD TRESTLE**
Bentley Historical Library,
University of Michigan
HS1661

21 **SECOND COURTHOUSE**
Bentley Historical Library,
University of Michigan
BL000297

22 **CLASS PICTURE**
Bentley Historical Library,
University of Michigan
BL001174

23 **ICEHOUSE**
Bentley Historical Library,
University of Michigan
HS1645

24 **HURON STREET**
Bentley Historical Library,
University of Michigan
HS1636

25 **CENTRAL MILLS**
Bentley Historical Library,
University of Michigan
BL000363

26 **SKATING PARTY**
Bentley Historical Library,
University of Michigan
HS1631

102 HURON STREET
Bentley Historical Library,
University of Michigan
HS1649

103 WALKER LIVERY
Bentley Historical Library,
University of Michigan
HS1587

104 HORSE COMPANY NO. 1
Bentley Historical Library,
University of Michigan
HS1641

105 MICHIGAN UNION
Bentley Historical Library,
University of Michigan
HS1608

106 HURON STREET
Bentley Historical Library,
University of Michigan
HS1685

107 BARTON DAM
Bentley Historical Library,
University of Michigan
HS1672

108 OTTO'S BAND
Bentley Historical Library,
University of Michigan
HS1691

109 EAST LIBERTY STREET
Bentley Historical Library,
University of Michigan
HS1680

110 HORSE-DRAWN CARRIAGE
Bentley Historical Library,
University of Michigan
HS1665

111 CIGAR STORE
Bentley Historical Library,
University of Michigan
HS1722

112 WALKER'S LIVERY
Bentley Historical Library,
University of Michigan
HS1692

113 FIRST CAR
Bentley Historical Library,
University of Michigan
HS1709

114 HURON RIVER
Bentley Historical Library,
University of Michigan
HS1662

115 MOTOR CAR #1
Bentley Historical Library,
University of Michigan
HS1664

116 CENTRAL FLYER
Bentley Historical Library,
University of Michigan
HS1663

117 CIRCUS ANIMALS
Bentley Historical Library,
University of Michigan
HS1705

118 BARNUM AND BAILEY
Bentley Historical Library,
University of Michigan
HS1623

119 COURTHOUSE
Bentley Historical Library,
University of Michigan
HS1591

120 MAINTENANCE TRUCK
Bentley Historical Library,
University of Michigan
HS1644

121 EARLY BIPLANE
Bentley Historical Library,
University of Michigan
2HS1655

122 ANN STREET
Bentley Historical Library,
University of Michigan
HS1590

123 CLASSROOM
Bentley Historical Library,
University of Michigan
BL000298

124 FIRE STATION
Bentley Historical Library,
University of Michigan
HS1586

125 FLORIST TRUCK
Bentley Historical Library,
University of Michigan
HS1579

126 HURON RIVER
Bentley Historical Library,
University of Michigan
BL000306

127 ALLENEL HOTEL
Bentley Historical Library,
University of Michigan
HS1659

128 STATE STREET
Bentley Historical Library,
University of Michigan
HS1638

129 CHECKING TIRES
Bentley Historical Library,
University of Michigan
HS1684

130 YWCA
Bentley Historical Library,
University of Michigan
BL000296

131 ALLENEL HOTEL
Bentley Historical Library,
University of Michigan
HS1693

132 THREE MEN BOATING
Bentley Historical Library,
University of Michigan
BL000308

133 DRY GOODS STORE
Bentley Historical Library,
University of Michigan
BL000951

134 PLANE CRASH
Bentley Historical Library,
University of Michigan
HS1671

135 VAN'S MARINE BAND
Bentley Historical Library,
University of Michigan
BL000811

136 TORNADO DAMAGE
Bentley Historical Library,
University of Michigan
HS1677

138 CAMP BIRKET
Bentley Historical Library,
University of Michigan
HS1585

139 REO AUTOMOBILES
Bentley Historical Library,
University of Michigan
HS1616

140 HERTLER BROS.
Bentley Historical Library,
University of Michigan
HS1697

141 RED CROSS CHAPTER
Bentley Historical Library,
University of Michigan
BL003665

142 ARMISTICE DAY
Bentley Historical Library,
University of Michigan
BL000815

143 EHNIS MARCHING BAND
Bentley Historical Library,
University of Michigan
HS1619

144 CADILLAC GARAGE CO.
Bentley Historical Library,
University of Michigan
BL000300

146 HURON RIVER
Bentley Historical Library,
University of Michigan
HS1667

147 EAST ANN STREET
Bentley Historical Library,
University of Michigan
BL000331

148 STAEBLER OIL COMPANY
Bentley Historical Library,
University of Michigan
BL003530

149 CHURCH SERVICE
Bentley Historical Library,
University of Michigan
HS1669

150 UNIVERSITY MUSEUM
Bentley Historical Library,
University of Michigan
HS1668

151 LIBERTY MEAT MARKET
Bentley Historical Library,
University of Michigan
BL003535

152 STEEL BALL COMPANY
Bentley Historical Library,
University of Michigan
BL000291

153 MY-T-FINE CAFE
Bentley Historical Library,
University of Michigan
BL003532

154 SHOPPING DISTRICT
Bentley Historical Library,
University of Michigan
HS1719

155 STAEBLER & SONS
Bentley Historical Library,
University of Michigan
HS1721

156 CHURCH OF CHRIST
Bentley Historical Library,
University of Michigan
BL003526

157 ELECTRIC TROLLEY SYSTEM
Bentley Historical Library,
University of Michigan
BL00325

158 MAIN STREET
Bentley Historical Library,
University of Michigan
HS1718

159 CLIMBING FIREMEN
Bentley Historical Library,
University of Michigan
HS1654

160 HURON STREET
Bentley Historical Library,
University of Michigan
HS1706

161 INTERURBAN CRASH
Bentley Historical Library,
University of Michigan
HS1621

162 VARSITY LAUNDRY CO.
Bentley Historical Library,
University of Michigan
HS1695

163 PONTIAC TRAIL
Bentley Historical Library,
University of Michigan
HS1593

164 LOWER TOWN
Bentley Historical Library,
University of Michigan
HS1592

165 ANN ARBOR DAILY NEWS
Bentley Historical Library,
University of Michigan
HS1652

166 ICE CREAM STAND
Bentley Historical Library,
University of Michigan
HS1584

167 COMMUNITY ORCHESTRA
Bentley Historical Library,
University of Michigan
BL005305

168 MEN'S CLOTHING STORE
Bentley Historical Library,
University of Michigan
HS1658

169 DRAKE'S TRUCKS
Bentley Historical Library,
University of Michigan
BL005318

170 MILLER'S ICE CREAM
Bentley Historical Library,
University of Michigan
HS1666

171 CLOTHING STORE
Bentley Historical Library,
University of Michigan
HS1650

172 STAEBLER OIL COMPANY
Bentley Historical Library,
University of Michigan
HS1653

173 1937 AERIAL VIEW
Bentley Historical Library,
University of Michigan
BL001956

174 AUTO GARAGE
Bentley Historical Library,
University of Michigan
HS1712

175 QUARRY DRUG STORE
Bentley Historical Library,
University of Michigan
HS1651